THE
PLAY-BASED
ORGANIZATION

Leveraging Individual Creativity for
Organizational, Outcomes-Based Innovation

SANDRA D. CLEVELAND,
Ph.D., R.N., CNE

For information on bulk orders or to have Sandra D. Cleveland speak at your event, please contact Sandra D. Cleveland at: tribeconsulting4u@gmail.com

Library of Congress Cataloging – in- Publication Data has been applied for.

Published By: Pen Legacy Publishing
Editing By: Heather Asiyanbi
Cover Design By: Tamika Ink
Formatting By: Carla M. Dean, U Can Mark My Word

Paperback ISBN: 979-8-9872891-0-5

PRINTED IN THE UNITED STATES OF AMERICA.

FIRST EDITION

ACKNOWLEDGEMENTS

Always, first, and foremost is my Heavenly Father. For my anchor of ancestors who allowed me to get to this stage. To present people in my life who have crossed my path for a reason, season, or a lifetime. To my futures who always remind me that hope is key. Thank you ALL for the gift of YOU. Finally, to my fellow players: Play On!

DEDICATIONS

I dedicate this to all of the wonderful workers who have a servant spirit and strive to maintain a sense of fun in life but who are ready to make a change to reach their dreams—this one is for you. Cephus, Lena, and Lavalle—thank you for believing in me and allowing me to pursue my dream of becoming an author who helps others pursue their dreams. Without your never-ending support, this would not have been possible.

As nurses, we have the opportunity to heal the heart, mind, soul, and body of our patients, their families, and ourselves. They may forget your name, but they will never forget how you made them feel.

— *Maya Angelou*

TABLE OF CONTENTS

THE
PLAY-BASED
ORGANIZATION

Leveraging Individual Creativity for
Organizational, Outcomes-Based Innovation

Foreword

Dr. Sandra Cleveland is obsessed with play, and its role in organizational structure. This has been one of the most exciting aspects of working as her coach for the past two years. You might expect someone with such a passion for play to have a distaste or aversion to hard work, but in fact, it's just the opposite. As it happens, one of the standout facts that I learned from her is that the opposite of play is not work at all, it is a naturally fun way to learn. Why not incorporate it into workplace culture?

In that spirit, Dr. Sandra's insights have been groundbreaking. When we take out the spirit of play or neglect to ever invite it into work in the first place, we are guaranteeing that creativity and openness-to-challenge never spark. When you shut that down for long enough, what you end up with is disengagement in the workplace. I don't want you to get the impression that a person dedicated to play wants to eradicate work and the intense environments work creates. Dr. Sandra's research and consulting is instead inviting us to think of work and play as a team, because when used together, the combination enhances many of the most vital aspects within an organization. It just sticks.

Serving as Dr. Sandra's coach in nurse entrepreneurship, I was impressed with the concepts she was emphasizing at every step of the journey and utilizing in her personal path to entrepreneurship. I watched her put in so much work, but creativity was always the thing really lighting up her path. It seems that her work has not only provided her with a purpose, it's also strengthened and informed her own journey.

As you delve into this book, read it with a sense of unfettered wonder and curiosity, the kind you might've retired since your playground days. If you keep your mind open, I'm sure you'll uncover some gems to take back with you into your own organization. I only gave her the tools to assist her on the road to entrepreneurship. She did the rest with her innovative insights and research, so sit back and get ready to learn why it's high time play makes a comeback.

MICHELLE GREENE RHODES
Certified Executive Coach

Preface

"When you play, play hard; when you work, don't play at all."
— *Theodore Roosevelt*

Rebuttal: "Play is the precursor to effective work and innovation."
— *Dr. Sandra Cleveland*

There comes a moment, sometime around early adolescence when suddenly, what we love to do most and we spend an inordinate amount of time at is banished, squashed and eliminated. In the blink of an eye, something that we enjoyed and partook in with reckless abandon is no longer socially acceptable. We even go from talking about it freely and casually to barely uttering the word. That word is: Play.

It's an amazing phenomenon really – how one day we can go from engaging in play freely and full-heartedly to rolling our eyes at the mere mention of it, as if it is something so vile and beneath us that we couldn't possibly be asked to associate with the thought of it. We used to invite our friends over to play, knock on doors asking if our neighbor could come out and play, and suggest playing as a way to unwind after a long day at school. We even had rooms dedicated to this activity alone. But soon playrooms became game rooms or dens or just "downstairs." We then made sure to carefully reword our bids to friends as "hanging out" or "coming over." If what we were doing looked anything like "playing," we'd be laughed out of the room. And of course, if we were caught playing or talking about playing past a certain age, we were teased and written off as immature and lame.

But why? What is the big deal when it comes to play? Why has this simple concept gotten such a bad rap? And why is this one activity that once brought us endless joy, amusement and unsuspected education become essentially another evil four-letter word? Why have we given up this activity without a fight? And more importantly, how could the reintroduction of play completely transform and improve the landscape of our workplaces? What would happen if we took the stigma away from play, and instead focused on its value?

Play is hugely important and not just in the lives of children. It's an endeavor that works the very muscles that drive our ability to solve problems, think creatively, and form stronger relationships with those around us. Yet somehow, we've relegated it to day care centers and playgrounds, and would surely scoff if our seventeen-year-old told us they were going to stay home and play rather than hang out at a friend's house.

Before I explain why play is so important to hold onto as adults, let's travel back to childhood for a minute. I'm sure like me, you remember a time when playing was the best thing in the world. I remember this period of time clearly, and I can remember one time in particular that stood out amongst the rest. It was a field trip day, which was already one of the most exciting school days possible. Nothing was more exhilarating than a school field trip. You were surrounded by all of your friends, but you got to leave the classroom and do something new and outside of the routine.

For this particular field trip, we visited a maple product manufacturer. That morning we learned how to tap a tree for sap and then explored how that sap was converted into items you could eat, like candy and syrup. Everything we learned was intriguing and novel, but the best part of the trip began after the formal teaching part was over. That's when we got to eat lunch and play on the nearby playground. The playground itself was familiar enough, having similar features as our school playground back home, but it was also different in a lot of ways. Plus, there were kids from other schools who were also eating and playing at the same time.

It was eye-opening for me that the playground even existed. I had become so used to our "home playground" that I hadn't given much thought to where other kids played or what it would be like to play somewhere new. The exciting part was that when we did venture out, we not only discovered a new place that was fun to explore, but there were other kids we could meet and interact with. In fact, it seemed that leaving our comfort zone opened up this incredible opportunity to meet new kids that we would never have encountered otherwise. These kids had new ideas for games and new ways of playing those games that they freely shared with us.

It was amazing to me how accepting we were of each other. We briefly sized each other up, but quickly decided we were all good. We then worked together to figure out what we would play. Some of the games we played were similar to our own games, while others were brand new to us. But whatever we played, we had fun, and it was easy. It was refreshing and exciting. In addition, somehow without actively thinking about it, we also learned some lessons about leadership. I don't remember the specifics, but there must have been a few of us who made the suggestions and decisions. Somehow, we coordinated the structure of play, decided what games to play and outlined the rules of the game to which we all agreed. In other words, we managed to navigate a complex balance of power to achieve real results – something that lots of corporate figures can't get done in an entire day and which we managed in minutes.

This experience stands out to me because under the guise of play, I learned some pretty powerful messages. I learned how easy it was to get together with new people. I learned that there was more available to me than what I already knew, and that I didn't need to fear it. In fact, the entire experience was more fun than a typical day ever would've been. It seems that because everything we did was done in the spirit of play, the more challenging elements just sort of fell into place in a way they may not have if we were engaging in a more structured activity.

Imagine, though, what would have happened if we had been forbidden to play and instead prompted to sit quietly at our own tables and not to interact with the kids from the other schools. Maybe instead of free time, someone gave us all worksheets to complete that reviewed the maple syrup facts we had just learned. To me, this type of setup sounds a lot like the lunchroom at a company or even the breaks at a business seminar. In these instances, everyone generally keeps to themselves. They eat their lunches quietly while scrolling on their phones or reading books or magazines, and they don't interact with anyone around them unless in the most professional of capacities. They then end up going back to work feeling isolated, uninspired and bored. How is this an ideal model of behavior?

When we were kids not only did, we play, we learned while we played. We were unsuspecting students, but those lessons tended to last longer and make a bigger impact than anything we learned in the classroom. We didn't realize we were learning because we were having so much fun in the process. If we knew we were being taught, we might've shut down like we do in classrooms or during presentations. I mean just think of a simple game of Capture the Flag. You might, during your first round, try running as fast as you could to the other team's area to search for their flag, only to be promptly tagged and sent to "jail." You didn't achieve the goal, but you did learn something valuable. Speed alone was not going to get you any closer to finding the other team's flag. Once you get another chance, you might try something new, like sending a teammate as a distraction while you stole into their territory to search for the flag. This might get you better results. But even if it failed, you would simply revamp your strategy next time around and try something new.

The same goes for hiding your team's flag. You might on the first time around hide your flag somewhere close to where you also decided your jail would be. This means that the tagged members from the other team might easily spot your hiding place. They'd also be much closer to its location and could easily access it when they were rescued. If they win because of this, you'll quickly learn that you need to hide your flag farther away and in a less conspicuous place. These are just a few of the things you can learn from playing only one game. If someone presented this all to you in the form of a word problem, it wouldn't be nearly as effective as simply engaging in play. Through playing, we are able to absorb lots of skills efficiently and enthusiastically. They also tend to stay with us longer.

When you actually sit and think about all the learning that is happening in any instance of playing, I guarantee you'd be amazed. And yet, despite knowing this, we still write play off as frivolous. According to Dr. Scott Eberle, play brings joy. It also is vital for enhancing problem-solving skills, encouraging creativity, and building relationships, yet we will wrongfully assume that it's to be relegated to children. Are these qualities not important in adult life as well? What if we lifted this self-imposed idea and took the stigma off of adult play? What if instead of looking the other way when it was referred to, we actually encouraged it? By implanting this simple perspective shift, could we transform the architecture of our teams and organizations? Would we then be equipping our employees with a set of skills and abilities that would improve operations overall?

There is a strong case to be made for bringing play back into our lives and specifically into the workplace. In this book, I will highlight the importance of play and how it could have a significant role in our organizations. I'll discuss why we need play and how to incorporate it into our current systems in innovative ways. By the end of this book, you'll understand exactly how to evaluate and implement play at your organization in order to not only get more from your staff, but for your staff to get more satisfaction and joy out of life as a whole. After all, the opposite of play is not actually work – but depression. And whereas work would undoubtedly benefit a company, depression never will. With this in mind, let's go forward and dig deeper into the very important business of play. But first, let's talk business.

WHO IS THIS BOOK FOR?

If you are a:

- **Chief Human Resource Officer** who desires to help employee engagement and strengthen the employee experience to achieve customer and organization outcomes

- **Chief Learning Officer or V.P. of Talent and Workforce Transformation** who is ready to provide strong play and gamification-based learning opportunities through the employee life cycle

...THEN YOU'RE IN THE RIGHT PLACE.

Are you getting the sense that this book is different than others in the organizational culture space? I hope so. There is lots of great information available on defining creativity, the theories associated with creativity, and organizational culture overall. While this information is definitely helpful (I'll be sharing a list of resources for your review), it still might leave you with questions as to how to naturally inspire creativity and resourcefulness in the workplace. My hope is that through reading this, you will gain an understanding of what factors organizations need to consider in order for creativity to blossom. In addition, you will learn the practical knowledge, skills, and attitude shifts needed to feel more confident, efficient, and comfortable along the way.

This study is organized according to six themes:

- Organizational Culture: The Current State and Future Trends explores the local, national, and global influences affecting businesses now and that could affect them in the future. This information will help you understand how best to brand your organization as healthy and creative.
- Creativity takes you through the concept of creativity and its importance in the workplace, how individual and company creativity differ, the factors that either help or hinder creativity, and how organizations can most effectively foster individual, leader, and group creativity.

- Engagement focuses on the need for employees and leaders to feel engaged in order to be willing to use creativity in the workplace and their need to know their creativity matters. Essentially, engagement and creativity are inextricably linked, and you need them both to reach your goals.
- Tools of Creativity and Engagement: Play and Gamification introduces the concepts of play and gamification and explore each concept's connection to creativity and engagement.
- The GamiPHI Theory™ introduces the three main pillars of the theory, perspectives of both employees and leaders, and how those viewpoints help or hinder opportunities for creativity in the organization. You will also learn about the unique creativity cycle that guides individuals to move forward in the creative process towards organizational innovation.
- Cultivating creativity in the organization details the basic premises for designing an action plan to actualize the GamiPHI Theory in your own organization. We will use a case study to illustrate our points clearly and to serve as a guide as to how to make gamification-based teaching, metrics, and incentives a core part of your healthy, creative organization.

RULES OF THIS ADVENTURE

I know, "rules" is a very ugly word in a book about play. You're likely now envisioning your name broadcast over the loudspeaker beckoning you to the principal's office for failure to comply with some rule. I promise you; those are not the kind of rules I mean. But honestly, I do want you to know what you are getting yourself into before you delve into this book. The information I lay out for you is, in a sense, a set of rules, but the goal is enhanced creativity in the workplace. Just because it's a book about play does not mean that the information contained within is frivolous or light-hearted. It isn't. In this book, I make the assumption that organization leaders believe that creativity will benefit and enhance the organization, so it's not a matter of convincing you of that fact, but of showing you how to get that done. I plan to take you on a [working] journey that will open you up to a new mindset – that of the healthy creative organizational culture. But you need to remember, as this oft quoted line from a famous superhero movie says, that with *great power comes great responsibility*.

Another assumption for this book is that organizational leaders want to hone both critical and creative thinking for everyone within the organization. This book contains theories designed to help you think creatively in relation to the systems and communications you put into place. Use this as a guide to develop YOUR organization's processes. Don't get intimidated and give excuses that you cannot or will not take the journey if this is what you want.

There will be days when you are working on the content that you feel like you've got a handle on it. *Celebrate these days*. There will also be days when you are trying to work on the content, and you just cannot come up with the right words or actions and are left feeling frustrated. *Celebrate these days as well*. This journey is designed to help you stretch outside of your comfort zone, so of course, there will be days that you might have to go back and review some content, and that is perfectly fine. Stay positive - there are moments that you will struggle - not getting your teaching exercise just how you want it, for instance. That's okay! Focus on the positives and all the information that you are learning. You don't have to master it all right away.

In order to make sure that you are productively working to accomplish these dreams, I want to encourage you to create M.I.E. statements. M.I.E. stands for "Make It Easy," and is what we'll use to break down tasks into simple statements. Once you get used to M.I.E. statements, it's easy (see what I did there) to teach others in the organization how to succinctly state the goal of their creative ideations in this format. For instance, instead of the goal, "our department will improve customer emergent communications," you can adjust this to meet the M.I.E. standards and say something like, "our department will make it easy for customers to reach us, so we can resolve their concerns quickly and maintain our customer retention metrics." Do you see the difference in these two goals? In the latter, you have turned a vague idea into something that is specific and realistic enough for you to complete. You've also identified the potential outcomes gained from fulfilling that goal.

Education does not have to be stuffy or serious to be effective. But know that while a relaxed attitude is desired with this book, I really want you to take the concepts you learn here seriously. If you do, I believe you can actively curate creative opportunities within your organization, and make some powerful changes to your company culture, and even to your bottom line.

Finally, HAVE FUN! You're taking steps to realize this dream on behalf of your organization. I'm here only as your guide and teacher. Take this as an opportunity to see your vision formatted into a plan. Once you are able to implement that plan, imagine how proud you'll feel to have been a key contributor in helping your employees engage, reengage and infuse creativity into the workplace.

You can use this book much like you would at a gas station. Typically, when you go to the gas station, you are responsible for the tasks needed to get your car up and moving again (i.e., self-

24

service). However, some of you may remember the days when you could pull in the gas station and have an attendant come out and fill your gas tank, check your oil, clean your windshield, and perform other tasks at your request (i.e., full-service). This book can be used in much the same way. You can go through all the material and "self-serve." This means you can use the information outlined within to create your own systems; you'll also be able to access a full community where you can connect with other members. Alternatively, you can reach out and connect with me directly for a more full-service experience where I walk you through what we discuss here and provide more hands-on guidance.

Yes, that's right, I said community. For anyone reading this book, I have created a dedicated LinkedIn Community as a resource for support. *I do not want you to feel like you are in a silo or doing this alone.* Therefore, you will see information at the end of this book on how to join the free and exclusive 'The Play-Based Organization' LinkedIn group. Here, you'll gain access to a community of like-minded individuals at different stages of the journey toward becoming a healthy, creative organization. During your journey, you'll be asked to post in the community. Don't skip this! Gaining feedback from your colleagues is part of the learning process. There are also those of you who desire full service – I've got you covered there as well. You have the opportunity to experience my, "The Play-Based Organization'" presentation. In addition, you may choose to consult with me and my tribe of experts.

When done right, adult play, games, and creativity are the concepts that cut through the noise and ignite true innovation.

Still with me? Excellent. Let's get down to the business of play.

Organizational Culture

Before we dive into the essence of this book, let's briefly introduce four broad concepts that need to be discussed in more depth in order to impact employee engagement and organizational outcomes most effectively. These concepts are organizational culture, play, gamification, and individual creativity, and they are key drivers of organizational-level creativity, and ultimately impact business outcomes. Let's briefly introduce these ideas:

Organizational culture refers to a complex set of values, beliefs and actions that define how an organization conducts its business. Culture is shaped by history, customs, accents and everything we learn during social interaction with a particular group. Within a company, the logic will be the same. The company's culture will act as a behavior and mindset guide for employees. That is, the company's practices, habits, behavior, principles, policy, beliefs, and other factors will shape how individual employees behave. The organizational culture is not only related to the behavior of employees, but also the way in which strategies are implemented and how customers are treated. The organizational culture is responsible for bringing together a company's internal and external habits, behaviors, beliefs, values and policies. In other words, culture plays a significant role in determining what standards a company adheres to. A good culture can motivate employees and help them grow along with the business, just as a disorganized culture can lead to productivity problems, absenteeism, and turnover in the workplace.

Play can be a hard concept to define. Gray (2012a) noted, "Play involves a constellation of characteristics, which have to do with the motives or mental framework underlying the observed behavior." He later shares four main characteristics that we tend to use when we talk about play:

- It's voluntary, in the sense that you're not obligated to do it;
- It's flexible and can be changed or manipulated, like Play-Doh for your life;
- It's guided by mental rules that leave room for creativity; and,
- It's enjoyable and fun. If something fits into these three categories, it likely can be considered play.

The concept of *gamification* is sweeping through the business world, with companies increasingly recognizing this as a positive influence over the past few years. Deterding and colleagues (2011) defined gamification as "the implementation of game design elements in real-world contexts for non-gaming purposes." Gamification has been used as a practice in recent years in normal business operations. The notion of gamification relies upon the innate desire of people to compete against one another and themselves. Taking tedious work tasks and turning them into entertaining games can create a better experience for management, employees, and customers alike.

Creativity is defined by Dictionary.com (2021) as, "the ability to transcend traditional ideas, rules, patterns, relationships, or the like, and to create new meaningful ideas, forms, methods, interpretations, etc.; originality, progressiveness, or imagination." Creativity is a precursor to innovation, and the fires of creativity can be stoked in a variety of ways that serve to promote innovation and progress. When creativity is stifled, individuals accept the status quo and companies lose out.

Organizational culture can be equated to the bricks of a structure, while gamification and play are the mortar that holds those bricks together in the spirit of building a creative workplace. The architecture of the structure is the creativity. The themes in this book will expand on these four concepts, but first let's look at the current state and future trends of company culture.

VARIABLES DRIVING CHANGE IN WORKPLACE CULTURE

Workplaces must constantly adjust to changes in the industry and the demands of their stakeholders. External factors are increasingly changing the way employees work. For example, digital technology and innovation are greatly affecting 21st-century organizations in new and unexpected ways. The advent of new technologies is changing how we work, how we oversee our subordinates, how we sort the items we use, and how we communicate information. It's not just changing the how either; it's changing the speed at which all of this is done.

However, as much as technology is helping us do things better and faster, it's leaving individuals in the shadow, as there is only so much data a person can process in a given timeframe. This influx of technology can create situations where individuals are tasked with using these technologies, but are uncertain, ill-informed or unwilling to operate that technology effectively. As much as things have changed, one thing has remained consistent, and that's the fact that it's still people who make up the basis of our organizations. Individuals are the ones who perpetuate organizational messages and who establish the communications, processes and evaluative measures in order to meet goals and metrics. Without the proper training and education in place, the benefits of the technology can't be maximized. That's where it's up to human resources or learning and development directors to provide the necessary education in order to get the most of the advancements that we are making in the field. The bottom line, however, is that both humans and technology are vital to achieving the organization's strategic goals.

Organizations need incredible leaders, supervisors, and employees at all levels to complete things proficiently and efficiently. Machines and technology can't replace this need for leadership. Though we can expect significant benefits from our digital era, we must not forget that it will still be our team members and the way we inspire and encourage those teams that will have the most significant impact on our future work environment. No matter how advanced the computer or powerful the algorithms, there remains a need for human cooperation in order to get the most out of technology.

CULTURE IS BASIC

Why is defining an organizational culture so important? Organizational leaders have different opinions on this. To illustrate more clearly why it's important, I want you to think of a football team. A football team consists of various individuals playing very different positions. Some are focused on defense, others on catching or running, and at least one on throwing the ball. On one level, it's only really important that each individual performs well in his or her position. One could argue they don't need to know much about what the other individuals are doing or the overall goal of the coach or owner. If they all do their part, they will likely win games. But now imagine that there was more transparency and that the owner had shared a vision with the coach, and the coach shared a vision and game plan with the team. Suddenly, what just feels like blocking one person or making a run that doesn't even end in a catch, takes on much more meaning in the context of the bigger picture. The goal is not to do an individual job well; instead, it's something like creating more local enthusiasm by defying expectations, making bold plays and working as a team. By being transparent about larger goals, the team can come together and find greater meaning in their individual contributions to the overall mission. When an individual understands their importance and how their part contributes to the end goal, they often perform much better. The same is true in organizations of all sizes. It's easy to get swept up in trivial and menial tasks and lose sight of the why, but transparency keeps individuals throughout a variety of departments on the same page. Many organizational leaders already accept that company culture, particularly transparency in inside communications, critically affects their organization's capacity to realize its main goal and vision. Others haven't gotten to this point yet. They feel that culture has a very minimal effect on the organization's capacity to realize their vision and mission. In this book, I will focus on those more modest organizations, where this need is yet unrealized. As these leaders become aware of the important role that culture plays in an organization's success, they will need to address what they are doing to support a healthy culture.

So how can we develop that healthy culture?

1. Give Esteem to It – Manifest ways to guarantee that leaders effectively take part in developing and spreading a healthy culture. The way we correspond, collaborate, and network are changing. The culture must adapt to these changes.

Culture is fundamental; however, leaders still perceive it as a work in progress. A social change will be required over the following five years, as just a few leaders are totally happy with their organization's current capacity to impart and team up (Katt, 2009). Moreover, leaders are effectively working to provide the necessary resources for team advancement, an indication of culture's essential significance.

Leaders can make two significant changes to impact culture development at the organizational level. The first would be to set up more professional and dynamic designs and devices within the organization. For instance, do you remember LinkedIn back in the day? When LinkedIn was implemented, a big part of the goal was employee and customer adoption of the social media platform. What did LinkedIn do to accomplish this goal? Gamification was incorporated as an engagement strategy. You were able to share your accomplishments, earn badges, and make gathering connections similar to gaining abilities to which others who did not engage as much would not have access.

The second improvement would be to dedicate more employee time and assets to the new technologies and innovations that are being implemented. When you embellish the training, you optimize the potential for progress and improvement. If these two things are done in the upcoming years, productivity within the organization will spike. (World Economic Forum, 2017).

2. See Things from Each Generation's Perspective – Millennials have different needs and desires than previous generations. In order to attract and retain millennials, you'll need to think about what works for them, not what has worked in the past. This means organizations should put more prominent attention on supporting and fostering employees' families, making the work itself more fascinating and intentional, and building an environment that is adaptable and empowering. Collaboration is huge, and all team members should be able to trade thoughts openly.

But this concept is not only reserved for millennials. It's important to remember that the workforce consists of a wide array of people across multiple generations, and it's important to make sure that everyone is heard, seen and respected. It can be easy for older individuals to feel out-of-place amidst many technological advances or the introduction of too many new policies. This is not a reason to avoid change, but to simply acknowledge how change will be viewed across many different perspectives and to account and allow for those disparities.

How we correspond, collaborate, and network will continue to evolve over the next years and decades, and it's important to adapt the workplace and culture to these new forms of technology while keeping in mind the people who are using these vehicles of communication.

Employees accept and reject job offers based on the technology and innovation that exist in and around the workplace. When you can empower collaboration and networking through the adoption of new technologies and avenues, you begin to create a culture of

33

creativity. When you can integrate these technologies adjacent to and outside of the workplace, you help ensure that even in an age of remote work that employees are still maintaining the social aspects of collaborating and interacting with colleagues. Make smart choices with the specific forms of technology that you adopt, and keep in mind that everyone in your employ needs to feel comfortable with these choices.

3. Keep Tools and Technology Inclusive – Building off the previous point, it's important to remember that technology is becoming increasingly important in our modern workplaces, but don't forget that people are still required to use and interact with that technology. New digital tools are drastically changing how we utilize our screen time. The future working environment will prompt us to change how we communicate and work together, and these digital tools will become basic empowering influences for expanded culturally diverse joining. As we move forward, the different software and programs used in daily work will evolve to become more culturally-friendly and will gradually promote more cross-culture collaboration. This is only going to become standard in the next five to ten years. Collaboration is a cornerstone to modern business and innovation. It will serve to fortify relationships now and going forward. That's why it's important for you to keep in mind the people who will use the technologies you select.

Also, as I mentioned earlier, tools are not the primary goal. The goal is the effect that these tools will have on your organization and culture. As organizations move from email to different devices for imparting, teaming up, and interfacing, management needs to remember that tools must always work to foster the right social setting amongst staff. It's still up to the administrators and leaders to create an environment that empowers collaboration through whatever particular technologies are chosen. If the technology alienates certain individuals or populations, collaboration and reception will be hampered.

4. Think About Real-World Use, Not Just Theories – Often the decisions about which devices, technologies and programs will be used within an organization come from the top down. The inherent problem with this idea is that the top-level executives usually have very little hands-on experience with using these technologies in the field. What sounds good in theory is not always feasible in reality. For this reason, it's important to consider the opinions of the employees tasked with using the technology that is being implemented. Be open to feedback and suggestions. When staff are forced to adopt and use a technology that makes their life more difficult, doesn't address all of their needs or creates extra steps with no clear benefit, it sets the stage for resentment and distrust. Taking the time to solicit feedback from the members of your team who are actively using these technologies on a daily basis is a simple way to develop rapport and to show that their needs matter. By creating this more collaborative environment where decisions are not made in a vacuum, cultivates a culture that is not only pleasant to work in, it's more productive. No good comes from implementing technology that is flashy but doesn't satisfy the needs of the individuals using it. Maybe something can be acceptable as a short-term solution, but with the feedback of the individuals on the ground, the current situation can be improved and perfected so that it is a complete solution.

5. Maintain a Healthy Social Environment – Leaders can frequently belittle the advantages of social tools at work. Instead it's important that they are taught how to utilize collaboration and business social instruments to improve correspondence, collaboration, and availability.

At the highest point of organizations, managers, especially in bigger organizations, perceive both that the future of work will be different from how things have occurred previously and that their jobs need to adjust to the new organizational environments they will be driving.

How we work in the future will be more interconnected, versatile, collective, continuous, and liquid, but at the same time, with remote work becoming prevalent, it will simultaneously feel more solitary and isolated. This less structured environment can easily become chaotic, befuddling, or overpowering, and it can also create a sense of distance that isn't easily remedied. When people connect primarily through screens and calls, it can be difficult to establish real relationships and rapport with colleagues. This will require better and various approaches to impart, team up, and network. Huge multi-nodal fluid networks will depend on creating new pathways for data to be traded and exercises shared. In short, technology will be called upon to lift the heavy burden of helping us form real connections

One excellent vehicle for this is social media. Currently, social media is a useful way for individuals to connect and communicate as part of a group. As we progress into the future, social media's role in business might grow. This is a way to integrate the social piece into a business interaction. This would happen naturally if we were all working in the same building during the same hours and in the same time zone, but as this becomes less the norm, we will need to create ways to create this connection virtually. Social media is just one example. We are all getting more and more connected with those far away from us, but something is still lost when physical interaction is reduced or eliminated. Creating channels for social communication will become a bigger part of company culture as go forward.

Current State of Company Culture

I t is more essential than at any other time in recent memory for organizations to involve employees in the current workplace cultures. What drew in and held employees in the past no longer resonates with the current workforce. Today's employees are looking for something else in a corporate culture. They respond to things like, more opportunities for professional development, serious instruction in their chosen fields, more comprehensive collaboration, more authentic hierarchies and greater transparency, a culture of adaptability, and greater autonomy and respect. When these qualities are missing in their current role, they are not afraid to leave their current positions to discover it. In our current culture, employees have access to much more information about competitors and the cultures and benefits within those companies. It's no longer the norm to find a company and then stay loyal to that employer despite some flaws in the culture. Instead, if employees aren't getting what they need, they look elsewhere. That's why it's important to constantly re-evaluate the culture as it's perceived by its employees.

As you prepare to investigate the culture that exists in your organization, be ready to take an honest look at what you see. Your appraisal of the culture may pleasantly surprise you or it may uncover some ugly truths. Whatever your culture appraisal shows you about the work environment, don't be dissuaded. Your culture is the thing that it is at this moment, and that's okay. After all, it's a place to start. To change, improve, or develop your culture, you need to see and comprehend your current culture as it is. From there, you can decide what works and what doesn't work. As you assess what you see, you'll answer whether or not your current culture upholds you in achieving your organization's main goal and objectives. If it doesn't, there is work to do. In any case, it's impossible to carve out a path to improvement until you evaluate your current culture.

Feel free to venture out. Diversity and inclusion endeavors have never been more imperative to accentuate than today. Racial and social treacheries continue to plague our networks and separate the general public. When it comes to the work culture, it's vital to do all that we can to break down the barriers between us and reinforce community for all individuals. The way in which a company treats its individuals never goes unnoticed. Professionals are constantly and silently evaluating whether their boss' qualities line up with their own and making decisions based on these perceptions. Accordingly, leaders need to reinforce their job as influencers of their organizational culture. Don't hesitate to take the lead on diversity or inclusion endeavors that are new, innovative and push the culture forward. An obvious, comprehensive, and positive corporate culture is the paste that ties an organization and its employees together. If you're part of an organization that requires some attention in the culture department, now is the ideal time to start taking action.

Some indications that your culture is in need of a refurbishment include:

- No one is actively focusing on reinforcing or assessing the current culture.

- The predominating mentality is that corporate culture is something employees should adjust to, not help shape.

- Leadership doesn't pay attention to employee concerns, sentiments, and assumptions.

- The benchmark for a solid culture is based on providing advantages and in-office conveniences — things like game rooms, cooked snacks, and yoga classes.

The first three issues contribute to a harmful company culture and can make employees feel that the business is in danger of a social emergency. In previous generations, the majority of individuals judged corporate culture based on the advantages and in-office conveniences offered. These methods today fail to measure up to the more coveted benefits of autonomy, transparency and respect. When given the choice between superficial perks and true involvement and appreciation, the latter will always win in today's climate.

Regardless of whether you believe you have a sound organizational culture or whether you think your organization can stand to make some improvements, here are five ideas to consider.

Sandra D. Cleveland, Ph.D., RN

1. Distinguish and Reaffirm What Makes Your Organization a Great Place to Work

Consider what attracted individuals to your company initially. Perhaps your organization was known for its effective adoption of technology and innovation, its commitment to work-life equilibrium, and a focus on learning and professional development. Alternatively, maybe your company has consistently integrated groundbreaking diversity and inclusion initiatives like compensation equity and prioritizing diversity recruiting, development and advancements as needed. Regardless of the specifics that set your company apart, make sure that these elements of your culture are not restricted to the orientation papers. If you espouse particular strengths in company culture, you must also deliver on them. Diversity and inclusivity doesn't stop after the final interview. Those same virtues must be present on all levels of the employee's experience or else there is going to be a disconnect between the culture you claim and the one you actually nurture.

It can be easy to overlook the qualities promised to employees when they don't seem to have a place in daily work. One would believe that work-life equilibrium might be less of an issue for this reason since countless employees are working remotely. Interestingly, however, very few people are actually prepared for the trials that working remotely brings. These are not things we were ever taught. Sometimes working at home and being in constant reach of loved ones provides the exact opposite of a work-life balance. In a corporate culture that espouses this virtue, leaders will need to adapt. This might mean creating additional training or implementing standards or suggestions for working at home effectively. To overlook the issue or to assume it's not in issue is not reinforcing the culture promised to prospective employees. A great way to reinforce work-life equilibrium might

40

be for leaders to urge colleagues to keep up structure in their day and to take time away from the phone or computer. Just talking about how it's acceptable to ignore a work text during a family dinner is expected and acceptable can go a long way to reinforce a correlating culture. Employees will see the value in working for a company that understands how circumstances have changed and make a point of talking about it.

Do what you can to reaffirm the tenets of your unique organizational culture. When you take the first step, it will send the message that you care about your employees on a fundamental level, and they will feel encouraged, motivated and inspired.

2. Record the Vision, Share It, and Invite Input

A few organizations now have a corporate culture statement that portrays, directly, the company's objectives, qualities and its expectations of its employees. Now is the ideal opportunity to return to this statement and ensure that the statements made still stand and that as an organization, these values are being carried out on every level.

Make a point in your record to discuss corporate culture as something living and not simply a theoretical idea. Then, at that point, highlight how you aim to maintain balance between evolving needs and maintaining a sense of consistency. For example, make it clear that employees can expect a certain level of reliability, but that as the world and the way we work changes, the culture will adapt to suit the needs of those who are a part of it. Sharing the statement broadly within the company, and even outside of the organization helps to clarify how senior leadership should deal with larger or more public issues. Depict how the association's center convictions and corporate culture establish the progressions and troublesome choices the business has made and is making.

And don't shy away from getting input about your statement. If the words are not landing the right way for people or if there are gray or ambiguous areas, you can only learn what these are through honest feedback. Input is a way of revising and perfecting, and is a great indication of how you're doing. Even the best-laid intentions sometimes go astray. Get the feedback you need to stay on track.

3. Standardize Open Doors to Promote Personal Connection
Telecommuters might be speaking with their colleagues like never before through email, text, telephone, video conferencing, and other collaboration devices. However, that doesn't mean they have mastered the ability to communicate virtually as individuals. Taking part in loose discussions about personal lives or outside interests is a new part of the social landscape at corporations that used to exist solely onsite. Now that many of us are working from home, the only way to have that connection is to somehow figure out how to interact casually via the methods typically reserved for professional communication. We must figure out new ways to make this a natural part of the work environment without opening up a boundary-less space that has superseded the casual workplace chat level. We can't simply do away with these interpersonal connections as this help construct brotherhood between coworkers, and contribute to a firmer corporate culture.

During or after group gatherings, make some time for employees to share individual updates if they choose. Video conferencing is ideal for this since everybody can see one another, but regular phone calls work just as well. You may likewise consider setting up a quick registration routine with your center group for getting up to speed and checking in with everyone. Using organizational, interpersonal interaction devices is another extraordinary way to share individual stories and updates. An example would be using exercise trackers to establish like-minded groups that can interact in relation to a particular interest. These sorts of associations can help groups stay connected; they can likewise demonstrate viable avenues for connection among fresh recruits who are looking to form relationships with their new, but frequently distant, partners.

4. Reexamine Your Diversity and Inclusion Efforts

Continuously watch out for opportunities to increase social diversity inside your organization by focusing on diversity-centered enlisting. Additionally, make it simple for all employees to take advantage of training and other occasions for professional growth, including oblivious inclination training. If you don't currently have initiatives like this in place, I propose leaders make a venture-wide arrangement of projects to advance diversity and inclusion, particularly approaches to help your colleagues embrace contrasts and highlight the extraordinary commitments that every individual brings to work. One approach is cooperating with outside organizations that advance the interests of underrepresented populations. Many of these organizations host or direct diversity-related events, including diversity vocation fairs, meetings, and workshops. Likewise, consider little occasions at your workplace that permit employees to share their personal accounts and experiences.

5. Try Not to Set It and Forget It

As explained before, corporate culture ought to be dealt with as if it was a living thing. When neglected, a healthy culture can deteriorate pretty rapidly. Your culture is not a one-time declaration to your employees that you can walk away from once you've created or presented it. Instead, you'll need to continue to discuss it with your employees and leave the conversation open as circumstances change. As your business expands and grows, you may find that this needs to become a routine. While it's a considerable amount of work, the rewards are worth it. You'll make and keep a comprehensive culture that keeps employees engaged, at the same time that you're helping the company stay dexterous for the future.

The COVID-19 pandemic forever altered our way of doing business. It's accelerated the concept of remote work and therefore has directly impacted company culture. But it's not the case that because most people are not physically at the company, that culture has become a non-issue. If anything, it's more important than ever before. When there is very little differentiation between companies since all the work is done at a desk in your home office, unique company culture is one of the few things that can help an organization stand out. How can employees at your organization still feel like a part of your brand, still feel connected to their colleagues and appreciate the unique benefits that they get by associating themselves with your company? These are important questions, and they are worth asking. The concept of culture is not gone. It simply has to be stronger than ever in order to reach through our screens and unite us.

VARIABLES DRIVING CHANGE IN WORKPLACE CULTURE

Three key components are driving this shift toward an advanced workplace culture. First is the rising assumptions employees have of their managers — driven, in huge part, by the millennial age. Recent college grads (millennials), who are currently the largest demographic in the workforce, are altering the landscape of business. Aside from the Baby Boomer generation, there has always been more variety in age within the workplace. Millennials, more than any other generation before them, believe that they should find reason and significance in their work.

Millennials want to work for businesses whose qualities mirror their own. Additionally, environmental and social equity issues are very important to them. Employees note that cultural issues should be addressed – approximately 20% of employees believe they've noted a cultural crisis in the organization (Harvard Business Review, 2019). Leader groups are observing these expanding assumptions as well. As a result, more and more leaders are seeing their organizations take on greater liability for cultural issues. Businesses need to adjust to meet these workplace assumptions, as they are turning into the norm among all ages in the workforce, including Generation Z, Generation X, and Baby Boomers.

Technology and innovation are the subsequent key factors affecting the shift to cutting-edge workplace culture. The ease with which information can be shared via emailing, texting and video calls allow for more flexible work game plans, since these advances permit employees to complete work from anywhere. For this reason, employees anticipate that their employers should react by offering flexible work plans. When this is the case, everyone is happy. Likewise, technology and innovation assume a critical part in the third key factor driving the shift to current workplace culture — the assumption for transparency. Organizations can't pull off concealing things from employees with everything reported on the web and via web-based media. Employees anticipate transparency and credibility and won't tolerate its absence.

Transparency matters since it's directly related to trust. Employees need to believe that their organizations take responsibility for their work and what they say. If there's doubt, it impedes the organization's capacity to advance and develop. Proactive, reliable, and veritable correspondence is at the core of transparency. Whenever leaders are straightforward with employees, sharing both the great and the awful, employees feel a sense of security and trust, which is imperative to being able to do good work. A modern workplace culture accepts technology and innovation, often thinks less about where and when employees take care of business, and makes a culture based on common regard, trust, and responsibility to meet rising employee assumptions.

WHY COMPANIES SHOULD CARE ABOUT WORKPLACE CULTURE

Technology and innovation trends are driving change; but business execution is the thing that decides a genuine social shift within an organization. The positive effect of a modern workplace culture can't be underestimated. It affects everything within the business, notably business results and key organizational measurements. Having a positive culture can go a long way for your organization. Below are some of the benefits you can expect.

- Attract Talent – Whenever an organization can put its positive workplace culture at the center of its talent-securing endeavors (particularly during a talent deficiency), it decreases the expense of drawing in new talent and builds its capacity to acquire top entertainers.

- Retain Top-Performers – Managers should react to expanded employee turnover by creating a workplace where employees seek to remain. Employees are bound to stay at an organization if the workplace culture enables their professional development, adjusts to their qualities, and supports their prosperity, among different variables.

- Garner Employee Engagement – Employee engagement is the measure of how dedicated your workers are to their work, and it's normally connected to basic business measurements like income and consumer loyalty. Organizations should search for opportunities to furnish employees with more noteworthy responsibility for work if they desire to improve employee engagement rates. Trust and regard are foundations to building a workplace culture that takes into consideration this independence.

- Enhance Productivity, Profitability, and Business Growth – Whenever employees are actively engaged, they are naturally motivated to work more efficiently and with better outcomes than if they are disenfranchised. In considering employee engagement, organizations in the top quartile of engagement have better client satisfaction, higher productivity, better maintenance, and higher profitability.

- Propel the Company Forward – Employees who are invested in what they do and feel confident in their role serve to propel the company forward by helping separate it from the competition. If workplace culture is fundamental to drawing in and holding ability, it is additionally vital to helping organizations elevate themselves in competitive markets. With a healthy workplace culture, organizations can draw in and hold top ability, cementing their upper hand. If an organization endeavors to be inventive, employees should be upheld and engaged in facing challenges unafraid of repercussions.

- Kickstart Creativity and Innovation – A workplace culture based on trust and imagination rouses new thoughts, technology, and innovation. Managers who esteem inventiveness and innovation see these qualities manifest more often in their employees. Censure ruins invention. When free thought is commonly shut down, employers lose credibility and employees lose trust in the organization. When free thought is encouraged and appreciated, it breeds more innovation and progress, which is generally a great thing in business.

The business case for executing a modern workplace culture has never been clearer. Effective organizations ought to be finding a way to assess, quantify, and put resources into a culture intended to bring their motivation, qualities, and growth objectives to life.

Future Trends of Company Culture

M ost would agree the cultural shifts experienced as a result of the coronavirus pandemic that started in 2020 have shaken numerous organizations and business models, overturning infrastructure and processes that have been in place for decades. The current landscape of business needs to be constantly evolving in order to keep up with the needs of individuals. For some organizations, this includes reacting to social equity developments, moving to full-time distant staff, deciding how best to help employees' prosperity, dealing with a crossbreed workforce, and currently tending to legitimate worries around the COVID-19 vaccine. In the next few years, it will be critical that workplaces focus on security and perhaps defining what a sense of normalcy actually means; notwithstanding, 2023 is probably going to be another year that is brimming with significant changes. While there has been a ton of spotlight on the expansion in the number of employees working distantly, I

Sandra D. Cleveland, Ph.D., RN

believe new trends are evolving that will impact the way we do business in the years to come.

GIVING A STRONG EMPLOYEE EXPERIENCE THAT HELPS EMPLOYEES STAY ENGAGED

Today's workplace is nothing like the one of even a few years ago, and one fundamental reason for this change is linked to employee engagement. The workforce is changing fast as new technologies are adopted with vigor. Employees are using these innovations to interact with their teammates and to facilitate their workload. Jobs are easier to come by than they were in previous generations, so the days of recruiting employees who are eager to simply have some work is quickly becoming a relic of the past. The focus of organization leaders should now be on inspiring and holding the top ability, but that won't happen with an outdated mindset. An organization's prosperity is profoundly related to its capacity to attract and hold onto talent; that can only be done by maintaining significant degrees of employee engagement throughout the organization. So what are some ways that this can be done? Let's take a look at some current trends in order to deduce the appropriate steps.

Trend #1 – Non-money-related advantages are becoming more appealing.

Prospective employees are craving an experience; they aren't simply looking to take on specific tasks. Because of this shift in focus, traditional compensation bundles that focus solely on monetary reward and benefits that have a clear dollar value are

50

becoming less and less convincing. Instead, things like increased job autonomy that improve employees' everyday experiences are turning out to be more compelling. In addition, flexible work hours and working from home have become commonplace in a post-COVID society, so employees have come to expect employers to offer them. Even advantages like paternity leave and wellness initiatives, that were once viewed as colorful, are slowly becoming more typical and less of a novelty.

Time has progressively become more important than cash for many workers, and effective employee engagement drives depend on recognizing this reality. It's no longer worth it to employees to sacrifice their lives in order to secure a hefty paycheck. In an age where you can literally earn money in your sleep via online sales and passive income, individuals realize that their time is actually worth more than money. While it might be easy for companies to raise salaries or tack on monetary incentives to employee packages, it's no longer having the desired effect on acquiring top talent. If you want to attract and secure the best workers, you're going to have to get more creative.

Trend #2 – Agile work environments are getting progressively famous.

Employee engagement isn't just about advantages and flexibility. It's also about the strategies and cycles that upgrade how work is completed. Mechanical and technological advances are allowing organizations to solve complex tasks by moving toward more deft work environments, procedures, and practices. This means creating overhauled workspaces that energize collaboration, facilitate stand-up gatherings, and prioritize left-brained activities like policy development and procedure creation.

Companies need to start positioning both the employee and the processes in ways that allow for growth and adaptability. It's not solely about the end goals. The way in which we get work done must make sense to the needs of the employees. Furthermore, this awareness can't be overlooked when it comes to virtual spaces. When virtual interactions are treated as though only the end goal matters, employees notice, and it sends a message that the process, their time, and their experience don't matter. We need to be deft and ready to reset needs or pull together groups on a more standard foundation.

Trend #3 – Employees long to make an impact and require more corporate social duty.

Progressively, employees need to feel that their work matters, both on a personal level and in the eyes of the corporation that they are working for. They want to feel as though their skills and effort are valued. This could be by simply ensuring visitors have a great experience or it might mean being a part of significant goals and initiatives. It's important for employees these days to see that their work somehow is affecting the corporate mission, and possibly that they are having a positive effect on the world at large in some tangible way.

Youthful employees, specifically, are longing for a sense of direction and hope to find support within their work environment. They function best when they feel connected to the corporate mission and espoused qualities. And oftentimes, this is why they would have selected a particular company in the first place. Corporate Social Responsibility will surely be a trend for the future as "employees are searching out organizations with solid CSR projects and opportunities to contribute. The businesses that succeed in the future will be those who can integrate social duty opportunities and who welcome all levels into the fabric of the larger corporate fabric.

Trend #4 – Organizational culture is king or queen.

Prospective employees need to know how it feels to work for your company before they are hired. If the organizational structure looks off-putting at the start, they likely won't engage with the hiring process much further. The prospective employees of today are assessing employee engagement before they even apply. They are not blindly jumping into an unknown culture and are willing to accept whatever it is that they find. As time goes on, employee standards are only getting higher. Employees need more transparency and responsibility from their managers. A few firms have an inverted pyramid structure where the main leaders are at the pyramid's lowest, instead of highest, point. They are nearest to the client and are empowered to make decisions that directly serve the client. When we create a remarkable employee experience, our team will respond by creating an exceptional client experience.

Employees are progressively looking for more transparency as a vital component of the corporate culture they choose to become a part of. Additionally, employees need to have a voice in how organizations are run. As the trend moves from long leadership and muddled progressive systems to revolving leadership and shared responsibility, we will need to make seismic changes in the organizational approach to business.

Attracting employees ought to be the main objective for any pioneer or organization. The key components for attracting top talent will increasingly be things like having a supporting manager, participating in meaningful work, and securing reasonable pay.

Sandra D. Cleveland, Ph.D., RN

Additionally, it's important to understand that employee hunger frequently changes based on the cultural values at any given point in time. Maintaining the archaic employee engagement practices of the past can be hazardous for both the company and for its clients. The organizations who will succeed in the future aren't reusing strategies and practices from the past but are paying attention to employees and watching trends to assemble an environment where staff genuinely enjoy their work and flourish.

Benefits That Help Employee Engagement and Productivity

"The system is tilted to favor the incumbent. The challenger needs support to find its footing. And protection of the new—of the future, not the past — must be a conscious effort."

— Ed Catmull, Creativity, Inc.

E mployee engagement – that is, having employees who are emotionally and psychologically attached to their job and the workplace – is critical for building positive relationships and performing well. A recent Gallup poll found that only 39% of the American workforce feels engaged. It was also found that highly skilled workers were 17% more productive and had a 41% lower absenteeism rate. Managers and companies succeed when they have employees who are submitted and connected to their work. But what makes engagement so important? What distinct improvements do we see in situations where employees are engaged? Many elements play into employee engagement, including how happy employees feel at work, how connected they feel to their colleagues and administrators, and how regularly they feel perceived and appreciated for their efforts. When these things are common and expected, employees naturally perform better. It becomes easier for employees to stretch or give extra because they feel appreciated and valued for that extra effort.

Employee engagement garners better results than offering regular group benefits. Benefits need to be a part of the package, but they are not the central consideration. More often, the group benefits offered are a corresponding feature to the larger, more central issue of engagement. When the overall environment is one of collaboration and respect, employees are inspired to go the extra mile.

Let's take a look at this phenomenon a little more closely and how it improves employee performance.

1. Better Group Execution

Employee engagement doesn't simply benefit just one employee, it has a positive effect on the entire team. Just think of a sports team to understand the truth of this. When a sports team has one or a few players who are negative, disengaged, and disinterested in the group itself, the team struggles, but when even just one member of a team has the ability to influence the other players for the better, somehow everything starts to work better. Engaged employees perform at a more significant level, and when those around that person experience that, it's natural to follow suit.

Employee spirit can be infectious. Whenever colleagues are surrounded by driven and inspired companions who care about what they do, they naturally start to care more themselves. It's the same phenomenon that happens when people share a common cause or goal. They feel propped up by others with the same mission, and a spirit of cooperation often follows. Singular engagement prompts group engagement, and individual execution improves group execution.

2. Expanded Employee Productivity

Well-engaged employees are more proficient and produce better work. Why? It's because when a person is engaged and connected to a cause, job or effort, they emotionally connect to that thing. The fruits of their labor is associated with their name and means something to them. It's in these instances that individual interests are lined up with the group and business objectives, and when that is the case an individual more easily can commit to an organization. When people have a vested and personal interest in the organization, they naturally are more productive. It's a sense of detachment or meaninglessness that leads to indifference and reduced productivity. Don't hesitate to monitor employee engagement in each face-to-face gathering. If you detect a drop in execution or productivity, it very well may be a sign of disengagement.

3. Higher Employee Maintenance but Lower Turnover Rates

If you need to build a high-performing group, you need to acquire and maintain a core team. It's difficult for groups to accomplish their best work if employees are continually cycling in and out. Whenever long-standing employees leave, they take important information and ability with them. When this happens, training new team members becomes especially critical, and you'll need to invest an appropriate amount of time, energy, and assets into your new hires.

A connected and fulfilled employee who's focused on their

objectives is less inclined to leave. So having more of these employees makes your group more grounded, more experienced, and better prepared to hit your objectives. In order to ensure that more employees are staying, it's important to have "stay interviews" with your team. These are nothing like post-employment surveys. The purpose of these interviews is to help you detect disconnected employees before they are ready to leave. Make it a habit to understand what makes your employees want to stay with your organization, what you could be doing better, and if there are any current concerns.

4. Accomplishing Group Objectives

Employee engagement plays a huge part in your group's prosperity and accomplishments. As an administrator, it's important to concentrate on your group's objectives. However, when you shift your concentration towards employee engagement, the change in perspective has an immediate, positive effect on your objectives. The reason is that colleagues who put stock in the vision will naturally work toward the set objectives. They will utilize their time in working toward the goals and their values will be aligned with the company values, so they won't hit resistance because their goals and the company goals are at odds with each other.

5. Lower Non-Attendance Rates

Engaged employees come to work and show up completely. Withdrawn employees have a tendency to miss days and are less inclined to be completely present when they are physically on the job. When your team arrives at work each day, energized, committed and prepared to work, it makes it simpler to advance, hit objectives, and perform at the most significant level.

Connect with employees when you notice changes in their

conduct. By taking small actions early on, you can hopefully avert any larger disengagement issues. When you notice individuals taking more days off or becoming less apt to participate in group gatherings, it could be a warning sign that there is a bigger problem at work. Try not to come from a position of dissatisfaction or judgment and instead approach the individual from a position of care and concern. It's possible that your concern will help an individual get back on track, or it might be totally unrelated to the job itself. Either way, you've shown genuine concern for an employee's well-being, and that action alone will go a long way toward building trust and respect. If it is something that is in your power to address, take the appropriate action.

6. Less Ruinous Workplace Stress

Both connected employees and withdrawn employees can fall victim to workplace stress. The difference is that these employees handle it differently, and a connected employee is easier to help than one who is already checked out. The result of work-related stresses can be diverse across your team, and these reactions will often be related to engagement levels and the disposition of the managers in charge. For connected employees with steady administrators, some pressure at work can be simpler to oversee and help. When you take the time to help an individual address the problem, he or she knows they're in good company and will feel empowered to confront difficulties.

However, if formerly solid engagement is lost, it can prompt the kind of stress that can impede an individuals' prosperity. This is particularly evident when employees don't feel upheld in their roles. Individuals can't function at their best when they're worried stressed beyond the normal thresholds. Be aware of when and how you push individuals. Stress can be an indication that we're near the edge of something stunning, but we need the right tools and resources around us to realize this. If we're simply worked until we break, we might lose the opportunity for a breakthrough. Ensure your colleagues realize that you have them covered and that pressure is healthy if it's moving them forward.

7. Lower Hazard of Burnout

Employee burnout, which the World Health Organization characterizes as an "occupational phenomenon … coming about because of persistent workplace stress that has not been effectively overseen," is perhaps the greatest issue confronting the present workforce.

Whenever employees arrive at burnout, it has real consequences – for them, for your group, and your organization. Burnout is the result of improperly managed stress. By keeping your employees engaged in their work and regularly taking the temperature of your group's emotions, you can lower the risk of burnout among your team.

Pay special attention to these burnout side effects:

- Physical and mental depletion
- Lowered productivity
- Decreased feeling of achievement
- Decreased work fulfillment
- And, you guessed it: Lack of engagement with work.

Professional Development Opportunities

Numerous organizations are combating this issue by rethinking the particular benefits and advantages they offer with the goal of retaining employees for the long haul. With the decrease in employee dependability and an expansion in job bouncing, it can be very difficult to attract and retain top talent. One effective strategy for retaining talent is to offer ample professional development opportunities. Per a recent report, about 86% of employees said they would change occupations if it implied more alternatives for training. In fact, Millennials rank the capacity to learn and develop in their given career path as a top determinant of whether to take or stay at a position.

Ultimately though, it tends to be hard to figure out what sort of professional development employees need. Before you put time and assets into developing a development program, be certain of what opportunities and learning avenues will actually be utilized.

Sandra D. Cleveland, Ph.D., RN

We've done some examinations in this realm in order to help you make those difficult decisions. Come along with us as we investigate the changes that could transform your organization into a covetable workplace.

PROFESSIONAL DEVELOPMENT OPPORTUNITIES THAT EMPLOYEES WANT

A new study showed which professional development tracks individuals crave most, including delicate skills development or leadership succession planning. The following are the top five.

1. Management and Leadership Training

Even though this is a general class, the impact of cultivating leaders is unquestionable. Competent administrators and leaders enhance employee engagement more effectively than any other measure, and as you know when engagement goes up, so does every other metric. One very simple way of empowering manager development is by offering online courses that can be accessed at any time in order to gain certificates. This way, professionals can take a crack at classes like Viable Assignment and Self-Management in order to add to their qualifications and to be considered for future promotions. Within these types of self-directed classes, individuals can investigate functional contextual analyses, take part in intuitive tasks and get support from devoted educators. Online classes additionally offer a compelling learning opportunity that permits employees to draw upon their work expertise. To bolster the online offerings, you can also try adding some in-person opportunities as well. You might try facilitating inward workshops controlled by significant level supervisors who share understanding on the topics at hand and can offer viable tips to their peers and colleagues.

Giving training like this could help foster trust in your administrators and affect employees across your organization.

2. Professional Certifications

Like management training, professional accreditations can incorporate course work while requiring more readiness and regularly including normalized testing. Accreditations are great midway options that don't take the same degree of responsibility as pursuing degrees, but still elevate an individual's skill set in a measurable way. This makes them interesting and attainable for employees moving into new jobs or taking on extra obligations. Schools offer certificate arrangement courses that can assist employees with getting test-ready, while also helping them to acquire the appropriate Continuing Education Units (CEUs). One great alternative for general business development in practically any industry is a Human Resources Certification Exam Preparation Course. As you assess which choices are best for your employees and organization, be certain not to mess up affirmation planning with authentication programs. While affirmation planning frequently includes independent examination, an authentication includes different courses that can be moved into degree projects like an expert. In other words, authentication programs are designed to enhance the current job skills that move the employee towards proficiency.

3. Technical Skills Training

While certain industries have a greater need for technical skills training than others, workers in various occupations are keen on propelling their capability in regions like programming dialects, site design improvement, and 3D embellishment. These training opportunities incorporate employees who work in:

- Art and Planning
- Maintenance and Upkeep
- Science and Biotech
- Media and Distribution
- Architecture and Design
- Information Technology and Innovation

Technical training can be incorporated as a part of affirmation prerequisites, workshops, or as individual classes. There is no one way to integrate technical training into your organization. For instance, you can offer an online course in information science for those hoping to take their investigation skills to a higher level. Alternatively, you could proposition individuals with existing experience to host a workshop for any individuals who want to expand their skill set. As businesses expand into new technology and innovations, it's great to remember that IT certificates can go far toward pushing your staff to stay cutthroat. Rather than re-appropriating undertakings, offer technical training periodically to keep and then retain ability in-house.

4. Teamwork and Relational Skills Training

It might seem like putting resources into technical skills is the most reasonable thing to do, yet don't neglect delicate skills. Abilities like keen insight, correspondence, and collaboration are comparably significant. These are the kinds of skills that keep your areas of expertise flourishing. While a few pundits may contend that these skills can't be taught, there are solid and proven approaches to foster these abilities in your staff with the right training. Coaching on many everyday activities can help workers to improve their correspondence, collaboration, and imaginative reasoning.

5. Manager Financed Degrees

For some employees, help with educational costs would be the most effective form of professional development. This can be more costly than other options, but the profit from the venture (ROI) may be exponential. Between diminished turnover rates, expanded employee engagement, and lower enrollment costs, educational cost advantage projects can save your organization a ton of cash over the long haul.

Besides, you might not need to spend as much on educational costs as you would suspect. There are generous tax exemptions that help to defray the cost of such programs. When you weigh the cost and benefits, you might find that it makes financial sense. Professional development is about more than simply meeting the benchmark rules that have been in existence for the past decades. It's about creating an environment that supports growth and urges employees to be their best selves at the workplace. When they show up completely, they not only help the institution that helped them, but they ultimately improve themselves. They'll recognize that as the valuable gift it is and will most often put their newly gained knowledge to work for your establishment. There will always be people who use and abuse the system, but the positives generally outweigh the negatives.

LEADERS' SUCCESSION PLANNING

A leadership succession technique is a method for distinguishing and creating inner individuals to fill key business leadership positions in the company. Replacements might be genuinely prepared to do the work (temporary replacements) or seen as having longer-term potential (long haul replacements).

Organizations effectively executing succession development to fill high level positions share normal characteristics. They tend to:

- Have a conventional cycle set up for distinguishing people who will probably expect leadership roles in the future.
- Provide professional tracks for high-potential people that are independent of those for expected leaders.
- Accelerate the leadership development of high-possibility leaders.
- Deliberately fill central management positions with inner competitors as a component of their successful development technique.
- Promote CEOs from the inside if possible.

These characteristics enable succession planning to focus on ability management as a way of building the future of the organization. It ends up being more "development-situated" rather than just a plan of substitution. Leadership succession is an effective method for attracting and retaining gifted leaders. You should be compelled to spot holes in your leadership ability pipeline and work diligently to train individuals to step into these openings. By planning ahead, you'll be enabling the company with a system that ensures the perfect individuals are moving into the perfect leadership jobs at the perfect time, and that holes are spotted early.

By combining succession planning and leadership development, you ensure that you're replenishing the skills needed for senior management positions while promoting a learning system that assists managers with fostering those skills. While succession planning for the most part, centers around a couple of positions at the very top of your organization, leadership development typically starts in middle management. By uniting the two capacities into a solitary way of thinking, you allow the organization to educate individuals on a broader scale, giving more opportunity to the hardest and most engaged workers. Succession development needs to focus on key part positions, which are crucial for the health of the organization. They're typically hard to fill but are essential for the future of the establishment. By observing the pipeline for these jobs, organizations can zero in on development drives to guarantee a sufficient stockpile of useful ability. The outcome is a pool of potential replacements as opposed to a couple of driving competitors. Make it straightforward to improve degrees of consistency and oversee wearing-down rates.

Flexible Work Environment (The Post-COVID Workplace)

The 2020 COVID-19 pandemic introduced flexible work plans, particularly telework, into the workplace at all levels. With numerous states initiating stay-at-home requests and permitting only fundamental businesses to keep their doors open, ill-equipped managers had to execute flexible work alternatives on the fly. Social removal requests will be completely lifted in the long run, and businesses will eventually return to the previous structure, but COVID-19 has forever changed the game when it comes to remote work. Employees' demand for flexible hours and distant work game plans don't seem to be going away. In addition, many businesses experience no dramatic lack in efficiency or productivity during this influx of remote work. In fact, some even found the new arrangement to be more cost effective. For this reason, offering flexible work game plans may turn out to be much more than the ordinary.

Indeed, even without a pandemic, flexible work courses can

improve enrollment and maintenance endeavors, expand organizational diversity endeavors, empower moral conduct and assist the organization's endeavors with being socially capable. Businesses can experience cost investment funds, improved participation and productivity, and an expansion in employee engagement when they allow employees more freedom in terms of schedule. Flexible work terms offer various advantages to both managers and employees. Such advantages include:

- Enhancing worker spirit.
- Managing employee participation and decreasing truancy.
- Improving maintenance of good workers.
- Boosting productivity.
- Creating a greater work/life harmony for workers.
- Minimizing severe effects on worldwide biology. Certain flexible work terms can add to supportability endeavors by diminishing fossil fuel byproducts and workplace "impressions" as far as the production of new places of business.
- Allowing for business coherence during crisis conditions like a climate catastrophe or pandemic.

PRESENTING A FLEXIBLE WORK ENVIRONMENT IN A POST-COVID ERA

Following a year that forced most employees out of the workplace and into remote work, the world has experienced dramatic shifts in how and where we do our work. This shift implies that organizations now need to re-visit ingrained work techniques. This isn't as simple as sending out a basic all-staff email with a return date. While employees may miss the kinship of their work associates, they've likewise become acclimated to having no commute, and staying in the comfort of their own home for breaks. It was awkward and difficult to manage at first, but now most people are comfortable navigating flexible timetables that let them oversee pandemic-related changes in their own life while simultaneously hitting their work cutoff times.

However, employees' dithering to return isn't just about missing out on comfort; there is genuine fear behind it. In an article found in a May 2022 article on SHRM.com, it was found in a sample of 948 workers that 21% were hesitant to get back to the workplace due to fears they'd get the infection and 17% of those back in the office weren't entirely satisfied with new security measures.

Even with a vaccine, employees still maintain their insistence on remote work, but there will always be a portion of the population that isn't immunized. Your staff may feel that full-time hours at the workplace are still not entirely attainable. For most organizations, the best arrangement is to offer employees a half-and-half work environment that blends distant work with on-site. This will provide assistance on the productivity front while still allowing workers flexibility to attend to personal concerns. Below are some tips to employ as you start planning for a smooth progression into a flexible work environment in a post-COVID time.

1. Allow Employees to Pick What Works Best for Them

Businesses are opening back up, and things are going back to normal. However, there are still restrictions and hurdles to contend with. Demanding that employees return with no thought to the concerns they are dealing with will only cause distress. Work with your team to establish what their needs are, and then try to accommodate those needs. The ideal approach to help your employees navigate this turbulent time is to offer "half and half" timetables. Let them have a say in what type of balance would work best in order for them to best handle the many changes and responsibilities they are dealing with. By letting them have some autonomy, you'll notice that they will be useful and remain connected. Partners need to address scheduling by paying attention to employees and organizing a flexible work plan that motivates certainty. Communicate key dates, reintegration procedures, and what wellbeing estimates you're executing to quiet their feelings of trepidation about being in an office.

2. Assist Groups with Adjusting Their Timetables to Encourage Collaboration

An additional advantage to offering flexible schedules is to offer groups a chance to adjust their timetables in order to amplify their office time together. We owe an enormous obligation to video calls, yet over a portion of telecommuters felt forlorn during the day, and many missed the social part of the workplace. You can achieve a more profound degree of collaboration on-site where employees can push and rouse each other. Figure out safe ways to reintroduce this. Additionally, group leaders can successfully arrange enormous gatherings and uncommon occasions when they know employees' on-site plans.

While the complete arrangement is the objective, a few associates may, in any case, be distant, either sporadically or forever. If anybody needs to go to a gathering, urge them to keep their cameras on. This will establish a more consistent work environment that causes them to feel like a piece of the group, regardless of whether they're in the room. Adjusting timetables and finding a way to advance inclusion fortifies relationships and drives growth more than partners requesting that workers follow a personal timetable that doesn't mirror "the new standard."

3. Focus on Company Culture

While working from home has positively affected productivity and engagement, company culture has assumed a lower priority for organizational coherence. It's been over a year since employees have appreciated group breaks, off-the-cuff work gatherings, or cheerful office hours. Everybody has to do their part to reproduce this familial inclination, particularly as numerous employees may be far off or dispersed. To modify your culture in a flexible work environment, you can begin by empowering more non-business-related gatherings during the workday, similar to a virtual game hour. Alternatively, you can get imaginative; anything that gets individuals talking and having a good time together again is an extraordinary advance.

You can go further and guarantee that any advantages you offer to on-site workers are additionally offered to those at home so that they feel like a part of the group. Whatever food-based occasions you have, for instance, figure out how to incorporate out-of-office workers. Turn the gathering cameras on for a virtual lunch, and when you order food for the onsite team, send out gift cards or delivery to those who are not in the office.

Group building exercises are also incredible alternatives to help staff loosen things up. Make use of video conferencing so that everyone can be included. Random data challenges truly get individuals' cutthroat juices streaming, while evening yoga helps individuals de-stress. A flexible-work environment procedure engages your employee while acknowledging any anxiety or trepidation they may have about coming back to work. Every initiative you implement should factor in safety. When you do this right, it will ensure that your team maintains a sense of security, engagement, and usefulness. Keep employees aware of your office's arrangements and keep providing this information and assets after they're back. Let nearby employees make their crossover plans so that they can feel. Zero in on office culture and ensure that telecommuters feel like they're still part of your team in every way. The adjustment period may be intense, but your staff will feel appreciated, drawn in, and, especially, useful.

Health and Wellness of Employees

Individuals are conscious about their health, and it is no big surprise that this outlook has progressively made its passage onto the work floor as well. Employees are striving to make healthier life decisions. They are doing this by becoming more selective about their food choices and by integrating more personal time to improve the quality of their life. For this reason, they will need to work somewhere where this improved quality of life is upheld, or, even better, supported by an employee wellness program. Interestingly, employee health and wellness doesn't isn't only beneficial for your employees, it's also an easy way to up-level your business simultaneously.

Sandra D. Cleveland, Ph.D., RN

ADVANTAGES OF WELLNESS PROGRAMS — FOR EMPLOYERS

MORE JOYFUL EMPLOYEES
Exercise triggers an influx of endorphins, or the "glad" chemical. Even taking a short stroll during your midday break has the power to provide constructive physical benefits: research shows that a 20-minute walk pumps blood and "feel good" hormones to our cerebrum and invigorates the imagination. In this way, by just engaging in a small spurt of activity during the day – as much as a round of table tennis – you can change the mental activity of your employees in a positive way, inciting confidence and improving execution. Cheerful employees are more useful, more engaged, and less inclined to leave – or require a day off. These qualities are more than worth the effort it takes to create them.

HEALTHIER EMPLOYEES
Another advantage of employee wellness programs is that they create a healthier workforce. Make no mistake; employees are in dire need of wellness programs. A Blue Cross Blue Shield report states that millennial workers begin to see a decline in their health by age 27, making them far unhealthier than previous generations were at the same age. A wellness program helps to create a culture of individuals who make healthier life decisions. Typically, it will improve mindfulness about a variety of lifestyle elements, such as, the food we eat, the measure of activity we get, and the importance of rest.

Suppose your employee wellness program puts a focus on exercise and food in the workplace. Maybe as part of your initiative, you introduce healthier options into the break room and provide workshops about the benefits of healthy eating. We know that microbes in our gut, which are affected by our eating regimen, influence our cerebrum and may even impact nervousness and gloom, but now you're helping your staff to know this too. What we put in our mouths for fuel affects us immensely. It impacts our state of mind as well as our physical body. This is another motivation to make food mindfulness a priority. When we encourage and teach employees about this, it improves business-related matters like absenteeism and increased leave rates while simultaneously improving their overall wellbeing

MANAGER BRAND

A lot is being said about manager branding and the significance of cultivating and maintaining a strong brand image nowadays. To attract top ability in a serious market, you'll need to provide something beyond compensation and palatable work hours. It's important to focus on your organization's learning and development opportunities and pair that with substantial employee wellness programs or initiatives. Having a wellness program is a major requirement for organizations looking to attract the best talent. As such, it's important to polish the brand as portrayed from a managerial standpoint. Employees are going to follow your example, so the top of the hierarchy needs to have a solid presence before you can expect everyone else to.

The initial two advantages we portrayed above for bosses are essential for employees: incorporate a tad of fun exercise during the day in order to promote joy, and put the focus on employee wellbeing. Keep encouraging this culture to improve the work experience for everyone.

An Equitable Work Environment and Opportunities

Workplace equity is an equally important factor in creating and retaining engaged employees. Equity in a workplace means appropriate treatment for all. The most challenging part is making sure that all your employees know and trust that they are working in an equitable environment. Transparency is key in achieving this; when the top-level management is transparent in their actions, it helps the team know and anticipate fair outcomes. When there is equity, there is equal opportunity. you show that you're committed to equity, you automatically create a positive work environment for both the employees and the manager.

Organizations should strive to implement a groundbreaking philosophy in this capacity and set their objectives to include encouraging an equitable future for their employees. We did a short investigation on the importance of equity in the workplace, took a gander at the differentiation among equity and fairness and referenced seven incredible tips to advance equity in the workplace.

What Is the Importance of Equity in the Workplace?
You should treat each employee with equivalent regard and poise independent of sex, race, religion, ethnic foundation, sexuality, or inability. Equity in the workplace is defined as providing equal access, support and resources, and outcomes based on individual needs. Equity alludes to approach rights to each opportunity and exclusion from any kind of separation in any workplace. Numerous nations have executed laws to drive workplace balance. It has laws to shield work candidates and employees from any sort of separation. Such laws make it illegal to separate dependent on race, shading, sexual direction, ethnicity, religion, sex, inability, and so forth.

WHAT'S THE DIFFERENCE BETWEEN EQUITY AND EQUALITY?

Equality is providing everyone with the exact same resources to do their job. Equity means distributing resources based on the particular needs of an individual. A simple way to think about it is if you gave three people on your staff step stools of the same height to access medications on the top shelf. This is equality. Everyone received the same thing; however, everyone might not have needed that particular thing. One person might be tall enough to reach the top shelf without assistance, so that person doesn't need a step stool. The shortest person, however, might need a little more height to comfortably reach the shelf and would benefit from a small ladder. When you assess the needs of each individual and then provide the appropriate resources to each individual to achieve a fair outcome, that is equity.

What is Diversity, Equity, and Inclusion?

The three fundamental terms-diversity, equity, and inclusion, generally known as (DEI)- are an umbrella term used to mean projects, arrangements, methodologies, and practices a company uses to make an equitable workplace and carry out diversity and inclusion programs. Advancing equity and inclusion as a piece of your company culture is essential for your company's accomplishment in diversity. The workplace is a naturally inequitable place, so advancing one evens the odds and goes a long way in cultivating workplace satisfaction. When true equity exists, you'll find that the workplace naturally will present it as diverse. The makeup of your team will include the best candidates for the positions, which will naturally encompass a blend of sexual orientation, age, and ethnicities.

HOW TO PROMOTE EQUITY IN THE WORKPLACE

Executing equity in the workplace is similar across all organizations. The goal is to ensure fair treatment for all employees. However, under the surface, there are subtleties unique to every organization. These subtleties need to be considered and allowed for as you develop your culture. Below are some simple ways to encourage equity in the workplace:

1. Do Your DEI Research

Before you take any action, you must make sure to have sufficient data. Know the set of experiences, foundation, and setting that you are working with. Use the tools at your disposal to identify problem areas and where there is room for improvement. Utilize the information and research in the DEI arena to get a comprehensive sense of the situation and what is in your power to improve.

2. Get to Know Your Team

Familiarize yourself with the current needs and concerns of your staff and review feedback over time. Gather applicable information from your team and investigate that feedback in terms of your company's socioeconomics, including your leadership group. When you gather the necessary information, you need to set the benchmark and measurements for the DEI objectives you intend to accomplish. The measurements include:

- Recruitment information
- Training information
- Advancement information
- Employee leave inputs
- Employee engagement overview

3. Set your Objectives and Install Accountability Measures

As an organization, it is up to you to shift the focus from the beginning of the recruiting interaction. Show transparency during the recruiting process, by highlighting everything from work prerequisites to pay equity. An organization shows responsibility in the DEI interaction by consolidating quantifiable results to remuneration, generally for the leadership posts and the general reward pool. This way, you will effectively attract a different, equitable, and comprehensive workforce.

4. Stay Attentive to Your Recruiting Procedures

Investigate the qualifications you are hiring for and examine the systems used to secure new workers. Take a look at where you're posting your work advertisements. Determine if you're reaching a diverse pool of candidates. Utilize both the web and real-world methods to reach individuals from each edge of society. When it comes to recruiting, utilizing solid DEI practices is a critical upper hand for organizations, as it assists with improving the company culture and ensures equal freedoms to all. Whenever you enlist a group of diverse individuals, you take a step toward establishing a more comprehensive and equitable work environment, prompting employee maintenance.

5. Hire for Culture Commitment

A powerful recruiting practice is to choose individuals who not only fit the job description but who also fit the culture. When an employee fits into the culture of the organization, they will have a higher level of job satisfaction, and will support the continued development of that culture rather than causing adversity and strain in the workplace. Seek to hire employees who match your company values and who carry varying viewpoints but with a commitment to the same objectives.

Ultimately, you need to hire the best fit for your group, not the person who only fits the job. Don't zero in on somebody's experience or schooling and ignore their values and background. An experienced employee may have the right skills, but a disposition that is only going to cause friction within the organization. Remain cautious when selecting employees. All biases should be reserved to whether or not they are a fit for the culture, not based on superficial qualifications.

6. Expand Onboarding Programs

As a leader or an HR manager, consider extending employee onboarding past seven days. An onboarding program doesn't need to end at a predetermined time. It might behoove your establishment to offer ongoing help and guidance for 6 months to a year. Remember, you are building your organization and developing your team to be top- level performers. There is no reason to cut assistance early on. When you do this, you'll guarantee your new employees are truly prepared to meet their objectives and make progress in their respective departments.

If you have workers from underrepresented populations, equip them with a guide for learning and development, and make sure they know they are supported. Make this a piece of your onboarding.

7. Encourage Leadership to Back ERGs

Employee Resource Groups, or ERGs, are voluntary, employee-led groups that strive to cultivate a diverse and inclusive workplace. They are otherwise called diversity bunches that open discussion for employees and can serve as a place of refuge for hot topic issues within the organization. Involving leadership in ERGs helps to upgrade your DEI in the workplace. Sponsorship from a manager group shows that the organization supports and believes in the mission of the ERGs and signals that they are their to help in any way. Leaders can offer direction, financial plans, tutoring, permeability, and networking to the ERGs as a way of showing support.

HOW WILL CHROs, CLOs, AND VPs OF TALENT AND WORKFORCE DEVELOPMENT EVOLVE TO MEET ORGANIZATIONAL CULTURE TRENDS?

The future trends for organizational culture will require a paradigm shift for the chief human resource officer, chief learning officer, and/or the Vice President of Talent and Workforce Development. The previous job descriptions of these roles focused on the tasks that needed to be completed – specifically on the monitoring of policies and procedures and in the role of administrator. These roles now need to evolve from task orientation to one of a value-added position. What does a value-added role mean? It means that instead of focusing on the deployment of the above noted content, the focus switches to the value these individuals contribute to the organization. Kokemuller (2021) notes that HR motivates workers to perform at the highest level possible and maintain an organizational culture of high morale. Individuals in these roles not only monitor the items put into place, but they will also partner with corporate and front-line managers in facets of change, strategy, and advocate/activist. These roles correspond with Dave Ulrich, a recognized Human Resource expert, in his piece "Human Resource Champions." Leaders are not just needed to accomplish tasks within the organization; they need to be cognizant of the employees' concerns, development, and contributions to their personal and organizational bottom-line.

What types of roles might evolve for these positions? This question was posed by The Cognizant Center for Future of Work and Future Workplace. They spoke with 100 CHROs, CLOs, and VPs of Talent and Workforce Transformation over a nine-month period to envision how their role might evolve over the next 10 years and determine what the future of HR might look like. They identified 21 job roles and descriptions as a result of this research. The themes that these roles fall under are organizational safety and trust, creativity and innovation, individual and organizational resilience, human-machine relationships, and data literacy. These roles of the future align with a number of the organizational culture trends already being discussed and are key to leveraging the employee and organizational growth desired to hone a healthy creative workplace.

Psychological Safety

I n recent times, the need for diversity and inclusion in organizations has become very pivotal to the success of companies. The reason is that most HR and even senior executives, from observations, have come to agree with one thing – organizations make progress due to the diversity of thoughts within their space. Compared with teams of people with similar backgrounds, teams made up of people with different backgrounds tend to have richer thoughts based on their differences hence having valuable perspectives that can be helpful to the company's workflow and progress.

Unfortunately, if employees are uncomfortable sharing their thoughts on situations within the company because of the fear of being punished, humiliated, or rejected, they would instead not contribute. Naturally, humans thrive in places where their voices are heard, and if that is not the case in their workplace, fear shuts them down. According to a 2017 Gallup survey, this seems to be prevalent in most companies today. The survey reveals that 3 out of 10 employees would rather not speak up because they strongly agreed that their opinions don't count in their workplace. If this is the case, we can infer that most companies do not adequately address the issues that limit good performance or underperform on a broad scale. When we're speaking of status and power, we are looking at the second feature of an Equistructure, *psychological safety*. The concept, coined by Amy Edmondson (2017), has been studied extensively. Adam Grant also speaks about psychological safety as something that employees need in order to feel comfortable and confident in providing their contributions to the products or the services that the organization delivers and the safety of their influence within this as well. When we look at psychological safety, which was the second component of it, we are looking at how safe do your individuals and your leaders feel within the, the organization structured the culture, okay, what culture is exuded in there? We need to make sure that folks are well-represented so diversity, equity and inclusion practices need to be incorporated.

This chapter will look at what psychological safety is, what it is not, the stages and strategies to psychological safety, and how it is key to effective performance in organizations. We will also look at its relationship with Diversity and Inclusion in the workplace today.

What is Psychological Safety?
Psychological Safety is a concept that one can share their opinions, thoughts, questions, concerns, or even mistakes without the fear of being embarrassed, rejected, and punished. Hence, Psychological Safety in the workplace believes that employees in an organization can freely speak up on their thoughts, questions, concerns, or even mistakes without fear of being ignored, punished or humiliated.

Studies and observations have shown that team members deliver at their total capacity in spaces where they feel their contributions are welcomed and valued. This way, employees are given what is called 'permission for candor,' which would mean that they are sincere about everything they share, and they don't have to bother being shut down. At all times, for employees to provide contributions to the company's products or services, they need to feel comfortable and confident in a safe environment.

In the words of Adam Grant, "Psychological Safety is a culture of respect, trust, and openness where it's not risky to raise ideas and concerns.' Amy Edmondson, professor of leadership and management at the Harvard Business School, stated in several interviews and speaking engagements how psychological safety is critical to a team's success. She would also say that speaking up may never come as completely automatic but should feel like the right thing to do in the workplace where you know that other colleagues will value your contributions. In other words, Psychological Safety should become a culture, not a one-time event. Why is this so, you may ask? I will share two reasons with you. When people are uncomfortable speaking up on some of the issues working within the company, the organization will lack the equipment they need to avert imminent failures. The second reason is when employees are not psychologically safe at work, they won't be fully committed. Hence, this will be a loss for the organization as it has refused to leverage its talents' strengths.

What is NOT Psychological Safety?
As we have carefully discussed what psychological safety is, it is also instrumental in discussing what psychological safety is not. Again, I will use the words of Adam Grant, and we will highlight them in fact. *"Psychological safety is not relaxing your standards, feeling comfortable, being nice and agreeable, or giving unconditional*

praise." Adam Grant

In the following points below, I will discuss the leaders' perspective and the employees' perspective.

Psychological safety is NOT about being nice.

A lot of people tend to mistake psychological safety for being nice – it is not. It is also not holding back on something that seems unpleasant. As we stated in previous paragraphs, psychological safety is more about candor. It is that you can make honest contributions and concerns and be valued by others for that. The fact that they will be honest does not mean they will always be pleasant to other colleagues, especially those involved in the observations you have shared.

Psychological safety is NOT freedom from conflict.

As stated earlier, a psychologically safe environment that thrives on openness and honesty will mean contributions will be shared that may not sit well with everyone in the room. This is based on several factors: members of teams have different backgrounds and hence will have different perspectives and approaches to some regions of the organization. With this in mind, the views and contributions of team members will clash most times but must be welcomed and valued, nevertheless.

Psychological safety does NOT mean all ideas will be applauded.

Employees at their workplace must understand that not all their ideas will be applauded. The fact that it will be welcomed and valued does not make it sure that it will be accepted or even used. Employees must understand that companies have goals and objectives. Though contributions to the processes and systems of organizations may be welcomed, they may not be applauded because they could pose a distraction rather than a boost for the company's success.

Psychological safety is NOT permission to slack off.
Many employees may assume that working in a psychologically safe environment permits them to be slack and lazy with their responsibilities. The purpose of psychologically safe environments in the workplace is that employees are more effective and productive with their tasks, thereby boosting their overall performance. In psychologically safe environments, both the employees and leaders of the organization get accolades for paying attention to their responsibilities. If an employee takes this environment to slack off, she becomes counterproductive, and the whole purpose for creating these environments is abused.

Psychological safety is NOT oversharing.
As much as your concerns, contributions, and thoughts will be valued and welcomed, understand that psychological safety does not mean you get to share all the information. Employees who overshare waste time and resources on irrelevant details hence deterring the mission of the company. The purpose of having meetings and gatherings in a psychologically safe workplace is to ensure that the goals and objectives of the company are clearly stated and sharpened for employees. Any contribution outside of this will be considered irrelevant and unnecessary.

Psychological safety is NOT the goal.
This may be hard to believe, but psychological safety is not the goal. Psychological safety is instead a means to the destination, which is excellence and commitment to high-quality care. For every company seeking to be excellent in the quality of the products and services they offer, creating a psychologically safe

Sandra D. Cleveland, Ph.D., RN

environment at work is the way to go. However, leaders and employees must understand that creating psychologically safe environments is not all there is to be done. It is rather one of the many factors that contribute to the high-performance rate of successful organizations.

THE RELATIONSHIP BETWEEN PSYCHOLOGICAL SAFETY AND DE&I

In explaining these two concepts, it will be best to begin by defining Diversity and Inclusion. Diversity and inclusion are interconnected but interwoven concepts; it is why you see both terms used together. Diversity deals with the make-up of an entity, while inclusion deals with how well the contributions of different groups of people are valued or welcomed. An environment may be populated with people of different races, genders, nationalities, and sexual identities, yet only the perspectives of specific individuals carry influence or authority. This environment may be said to be diverse but not inclusive.

Now that we know what Diversity and Inclusion are, let's look at what a diverse and inclusive workplace is. A diverse and inclusive workplace is an environment where everyone feels equally involved in and supports all workplace areas, regardless of their identity or occupation. The word "all" is vital in defining this kind of workplace. Once it is not "all," it is not a diverse and inclusive workplace. If you are an HR or senior professional in the workplace, ask yourself some of the following questions below:

- Do you have diversity in recruiting the workforce in your company? Is it evident in your departments or your leadership?

92

- Do you have a workplace where 50% of your employees are men, but 0% of your men are managers?
- Do you have a good reputation in relating with people of color but put them in the same department and under some customized rules?

These are a few questions that can help you indicate if you have a diverse and inclusive workplace or not.

WHY ARE PSYCHOLOGICAL SAFETY AND DE&I SO IMPORTANT IN THE WORKPLACE TODAY?

In understanding a diverse and inclusive workplace, we can now adequately relate it with a psychologically safe environment. From the previous sections, we can see the similarities of psychological safety, diversity, and inclusion (DE&I). A psychologically safe workplace will also be said to be a diverse and inclusive workplace. One of the advantages of having diversity and inclusion within a psychologically safe environment is that employees can be themselves at work without any fear of judgment. In other words, they can freely exhibit their race, ethnicity, gender, sexual orientation, background, family status, and all other parts of their identity, and they will not be judged or discriminated against for doing so. Research shows that when employees trust that they and their colleagues will be treated fairly regardless of who they are or what they do, they are more likely to do these three things:

- More likely to pride themselves in their work
- More likely to look forward to going to work
- More likely to stay in the company for a long time.

Having an inclusive workplace not only attracts a diverse set of talents, but the workplace will also help you retain these talents you have recruited because they find joy and satisfaction with their work most companies may not offer. Another advantage of diversity in a psychologically safe environment is the fact that it improves employees' productivity, boosts innovation, and saves the company time and money in delivering results. The more diverse talents you have on the team, the more potential you can unlock in them to meet the company's targets and goals and even exceed them. When leaders celebrate, value, and respect others' diversity, this will lead to a psychologically safe space within team members, strengthening the bond, open-mindedness, positivity, and possibilities within the organization.

THE 4 STAGES OF PSYCHOLOGICAL SAFETY

Organizations that create and grow a community of trust and respect for team members will feel free to collaborate anytime and any day. They will also feel safe taking risks with this unanimous understanding that it will enable them to implement rapid innovation.

In Dr. Timothy Clark's book, *The 4 Stages of Psychological Safety: Defining the Path to Inclusion and Innovation*, he describes that a psychologically safe environment has 4 stages that all employees pass through. Let's have a look at these stages one after the other.

Stage 1: Inclusion Safety

According to Maslow's hierarchy of needs, all humans require basic needs to be met to reach their full potential – the need to connect and belong. This explains why the first stage an employee goes through is inclusion safety. Everyone primarily values the need to be accepted first over the need to be heard. Employees want to know that they are accepted for who they are, regardless of their defining characteristics or unique attributes. The employee feels a shared identity in this environment that shows them that they matter and belong. When this happens, fear, doubt, and discouragement are taken off the employee and are replaced by independence and confidence.

Every employee goes through that first step of acceptance and validation. As they get to settle in that, they now go through the next stage, as we will come to see.

Stage 2: Learner Safety

Another critical need for humans is the need to learn and grow. The learning safety stage is the learning process every employee gets to. At this stage, people feel safe to exchange in the learning process, such as giving and receiving feedback and asking questions, making contributions, and mistakes. It is not a probability that mistakes will be made; it is a certainty. At this stage, there is still some inhibition of feeling safe to contribute. However, as the employee gradually settles in this stage, they realize the beauty and are more vulnerable and willing to take risks with their colleagues.

This develops resilience for the employee in the learning process. The employee learns both intellectually (with their head) and emotionally (with their heart). When the leader creates a learner safety for others, we give the employee an enabling environment, and in return, we see that willingness kindled in them to learn.

Stage 3: Contributor Safety

The contributor safety satisfies the need for humans to make a difference with their potential. At this stage, the employee feels accepted already and has also known that it's alright to contribute. It's part of the learning phase. At this stage, the employee now feels able to use their skills to execute the ideas shared. They are already full team members, and hence they want to participate in the value-creation process fully. The beauty of this is when leaders encourage employees in the contributor safety stage, they give them the green flag in maximizing their fullest potential for their tasks and responsibilities. Leaders should not micromanage employees because employees are limited when they do, and we don't get to find out their true strengths.

The more employees contribute, the more competence and mastery they gain in that field, and the more the organization meets its objectives.

Stage 4: Challenger Safety

The final stage is the challenger safety stage. At this stage, employees are now more confident than ever, and it means that after satisfying the need to contribute, there is now a need to do even better. Employees feel safe to speak up and challenge the status quo when they perceive an opportunity for change or improvement. This stage is the safest as employees can air their opinions without the risk of their reputation being damaged.

Employees are not humiliated but rather respected and have the permission to disagree with something that may not look or feel suitable for the organization. This is fundamental for successful organizations as it allows employees to be more innovative in their approach rather than everyone fitting into a particular culture or norm of doing things.

7 STRATEGIES TO CREATE PSYCHOLOGICAL SAFETY AT WORK

Now that you have seen all that needs to be learned in psychological safety, it is essential that we close this chapter by stating the key strategies to creating psychological safety in the workplace today. If you are not able to do all seven at first, that's fine. You can begin with one, and with time you will see that the others are also interconnected and will come to light to you and amongst your employees.

Below are the seven strategies in creating a psychologically safe environment at work:

1. Break the "Golden Rule"

There is the common saying that you treat others like you want to be treated. However, in psychological safety, that's the opposite. You don't treat others like you want but like they want. You must break the rule if you want to get valuable feedback from your employees. Deliberately take out time to ask your employees their thoughts and opinions concerning work processes in the organization. Great leaders would never operate from a perspective of what they want but what the people following them. Leaders know that they are primarily servants to their people, so they find out what makes them more effective and productive. This way, you are confident that everyone is getting the treatment they want based on them.

2. Promote effectiveness, not efficiency

In Simon Sinek's book, *Leaders Eat Last*, he talked about the importance of creating a safe and secure working environment for employees. Leaders should not have the mindset where they treat employees as a means to an end. Either that end is the company's financial outcome or performance in the company, leaders should think differently. Leaders should focus on creating a safe environment for employees to be free from threats and limitations. This way, employees let all guards down and are confident to deliver in that kind of environment. The bright side is that this will help the company be shielded from likely dangers outside and seize excellent opportunities as they come.

3. Give employees a voice

In the next chapter of this book, we will see what is known as employee empowerment. Employee empowerment gives your employees a voice, the right, authority, and power to contribute and make decisions when the occasion demands. When you give your employees a voice, you communicate a sense of ownership to them. This will make them feel even more valued and unlock some of their greatest potential to benefit the company. Some of this potential would not have been unlocked if there was still some limitation. Giving your employees a voice is necessary to show that they belong and are part of the organization.

4. Promote healthy conflict

We stated already that psychological safety does not mean there will be no conflict. Conflicts will arise due to differences; however, these conflicts don't have to be unhealthy. When employees share their thoughts on work-related concerns, others can always give their feedback on these thoughts in a constructive way. When these opinions are handled constructively, it will be evident that the one opposing these contributions seeks to understand better and not discriminate. One helpful way to also ensure healthy conflict is using the Just Like Me technique. In other words, for every contribution, you put yourself as an example to give more light to your contributions. This way, everyone gets to address these concerns constructively and healthily, ultimately bringing progress for the organization.

5. Earn and extend trust

Just as employees earn the trust of their leaders, leaders must earn the trust of their employees. Leaders show trust by integrity, being true to what the company stands for, and ensuring everyone upholds these standards. Trust must be built, and not only so, but it must also be sharpened and sustained from time to time. Trust is vital for employees to be sure they are in a psychologically safe workplace. Being an example of trustworthiness will inspire others to be trustworthy, hence growing a positive community of committed and honest employees.

6. Welcome curiosity

Nurturing a curiosity culture amongst employees makes them more present in the journey and more creative in approaching its objectives. When leaders promote a culture of eager and agile people to learn and inquire about things regardless of the uncertainty and vulnerability, a thriving community gradually takes shape. Employees can better adapt and align themselves to the updates of their approach to specific work-related issues, seeing that it is solved.

7. Think differently about creativity

Finally, in solidifying psychological safety in the workplace, use an unconventional approach to creativity. Unlike the way the world thinks, the path of risks and uncertainty should not be discouraged but rather embraced. When 'rough' or 'incomplete' ideas are shared without fear of penalty, other employees can draw creativity and inspiration for further development together. This does not only make the work of top-notch quality, but it also

Sandra D. Cleveland, Ph.D., RN

strengthens the openness and trust of every member of the team. Thinking differently about creativity is a great way to boost a psychologically safe environment.

Empowerment

The last component of equistructure is *empowerment*. It loosely translates into how comfortable employees and leaders feel in moving forward creatively and feeling like they have a say within the workplace. This pillar will be evidenced in employee satisfaction. Strengthening employee and leader empowerment is necessary in the equistructure pillar. Higher levels of perceived empowerment will ultimately help strengthen the organizational culture and health.

What Is Employee Empowerment?
Employee Empowerment is described as giving authority, power, resources, responsibility, and even freedom to employees to make decisions, take initiatives, and solve work-related issues where and when necessary. You will agree that one factor contributing to employees not giving their best at their workplace could be that there is little or no authority given to them by the management.

That ultimately limits employees who see issues and concerns they can adequately address in the organization. Still, because no one has empowered them to solve these concerns, they instead watch like everybody else.

Allocation of authority is based on the concept of trust-based relationships and not delegation-based relationships. It is based on trust in empowering employees because it is not a one-time thing but a continuous process. The higher management in the workplace sometimes makes the mistake of having all authority instead of giving some to the lower employees. This is usually because the management may have had to deal with unpleasant experiences in the past that hurt the organization and even its performance. Another reason could be that higher management assumes employees will abuse this power when given, so they hold all of it to themselves. This should not be.

While the management may think they are doing the company a favor, they limit the potential of the employees and the organization's performance. Research has shown that empowering employees is directly proportional to the increased productivity of the employees; there is also an increase in job satisfaction and company loyalty.

THE BENEFITS OF WORKPLACE EMPOWERMENT

You can never go wrong by empowering employees. The only case you can be wrong is when you fail to assign the right ones. As a leader, you risk losing money, resources, and even people by empowering the wrong employees. So, ensure to make the right choice.

In this section, we will see what the benefits that come with empowering employees are. Let's begin.

1. **More Productivity** ~ Employees will be more productive when given adequate resources, authority, and power in solving work-related issues and making decisions for themselves. Employees will never be excited to work on projects they feel they are not great at. For even the ones they can do, they don't enjoy being told how to work. No one does. When employees make their decisions, there is a sense of empowerment and productivity they feel. This ultimately creates a better work environment and makes them thrive in their expertise.

2. **Employee Satisfaction** ~ There is a sense of fulfillment for employees in knowing that they had autonomy in a project. This gives them confidence and competence in themselves for even future projects and challenges that may come much later. There is that satisfaction the employee feels when they know that the company's success was based on their input in that project. No other joy can replace that. This reinforces the message to employees that they are in every sense part of the team.

3. **Improved Employee Branding** ~ Employee branding would be that your employees have been empowered to have such a work culture that makes your company shine amongst many others. Employee branding comes with many benefits. Some of these are that the company becomes a hub of great talents because everyone realizes the company's productive work culture and environment. Another fantastic benefit to employee branding is that there would not be a need for too many recruitments. Some of the most extraordinary talents will already be working in your company, and they will be less likely to live.

4. **Flattening the Hierarchy ~** Another advantage that comes with empowering your employees is that you flatten the hierarchy. When employees are empowered, there is less need to have too many management levels for better communication and transparency. Although, this could be a disadvantage if not appropriately handled. There could be confusion of roles, and one may not correctly account for employees responsible for a project if it succeeds or fails. This can be solved by understanding the level of flatness you want and ensuring that though the hierarchy is orderly, it is still flexible for communication and transparency.

5. **Customer Handling ~** The satisfaction of every customer in a company is based on a critical factor: the organization's processes. If your employees are empowered, they will handle customers better, translating to good customer service. Good customer service always results in customer loyalty. Another great benefit empowering employees who regularly interact with customers is that customers who have specific issues or concerns can always complain to the employees. If the employees have the resources and authority to solve that challenge, it will save time, and the customer will be satisfied.

CULTIVATING TRUE EMPLOYEE EMPOWERMENT

After stating the benefits of empowering employees, it will be best to communicate the steps involved in empowering employees to have a positive work environment. Below are the 7 steps in creating and cultivating true employee empowerment.

1. **Build Trust and Respect** ~ In empowering employees, you must build trust and respect the values of your employees' contributions. As we stated in the last chapter, if people feel their thoughts and contributions are not accepted, they will keep to themselves, which will not be advantageous to the team.

2. **Facilitate Robust Communication** ~ Communication is vital in empowering employees. This should be done in two ways; the management should ensure employees are carried along and not be the last to know about certain developments critical to the company. In the same vein, the management should always give employees the freedom to speak and be heard. Leaders must value and hear the contributions of their employees. When you do this, it boosts employees' morale and empowers them to know that their contributions are worth it.

3. **Be Clear About Company Core Values and Goals**. ~ If any company is going to avoid assumptions from their employees, the management must ensure that the core values and goals of the company are clearly stated. This will help employees know what is expected of them. When they do, they can easily align themselves to the values and goals according to their responsibilities within the organization. When they see that their contribution is impacting the company's positive performance, they feel confident and empowered to stay the course.

4. **Offer Feedback** ~ Feedback is necessary for every company to keep thriving. They help for a good working environment. Feedback should be an everyday thing and should be taken note of and worked upon immediately. Often, companies

will request feedback from employees but not act on it. This will hinder productivity and not empower employees to keep giving necessary feedback. Feedback from the management should be taken seriously and worked on for better efficiency of the organization.

5. **Provide Tools and Resources** ~ In empowering your employees, do not just give them authority and power. Also, give them the resources and enabling environment to perform to their best capacity. If employees are adequately equipped with the tools and resources needed to complete a task, they will be confident to deliver. Not only for the present but even when future challenges arise. This is another way you can empower your employees to do better.

6. **Timely Rewards and Recognition** ~ When employees' complete projects successfully, it behooves the management to reward and recognize the team or department responsible. This boosts the morale of that team and every other employee within the organization to do better. It's a good motivation for employees to get the needed push to be excellent at their work and take ownership of it. This way, they are empowered to be better.

7. **Inspire Creative Thinking** ~ Innovative thinking cannot be over-emphasized. It is fundamental to the success of the company. Creative thinking inspires employees to think out of the box, especially on new challenges, and need alternative solutions to address them. This way, employees are pushed to unlock some of the potential they may not have known existed. Management should promote good thinking for employees where they proactively engage them in idea-sharing.

EQUISTRUCTURE EXAMPLE

Let's think about this example. One of the biggest areas that people tend to state as a reason for leaving their job is their manager. And so, as an example, if a manager is considered toxic, they are in fact polluting the healthy environment that is attempted to be created within the organization will either need to have strategies in place to help them emerge from this toxicity state to a healthy state, as well as removing and improving the status for the employees that are under them. Activity only goes so far as the state of healthiness within the organization. Health should not always be a reactive response. Health should be very proactive. And that is the case for an organization as well. Just like from an individual standpoint where we talk about preventive measures, such as nutrition and exercise to help maintain better wellbeing and better health outcomes, whether actual and or proceed the same idea needs to be taken into account from an organization perspective as well.

Think about the organizational structure. How are vulnerable populations in the organization reduced or eliminated? What changes can be made from different levels, giving employees the opportunity to help create change within the organization and beyond giving them that information so that they can make moves. The policies within the organization matter because policies equal organizational power. Leaders need to help provide access to employees from this standpoint as well. It is important for a level of openness in the environment to occur so that folks can help manage the environment as well as make necessary changes to it.

STRUCTURE 3: INNOSTRUCTURE

I addressed the first two pillars of infrastructure and equistructure. The third pillar that we are going to pay attention to is Innostructure, which incorporates a few components as well. Innostructure includes a two-fold definition. The first portion of the Innostructure is the ability of organizational leaders to hone and advance innovation based on individual and organizational values. The second portion of the definition focuses on the formal infusion of innovation in organizational practice. Please note – measures incorporated in the innostructure pillar should move the organization towards (but not reaching) true innovative practices.

Leadership Involvement
The first component of infrastructure is leadership involvement. We look at the levels of involvement of leadership to help employees move forward and the activities that they do to help create that creative environment in the first one. This place to help provide any necessary resources to help their employees move forward, to provide avenues that their employees can get involved in.

Leadership Flexibility
The second component of the infrastructure is leadership flexibility. Part of it is going to be the strength of changing and adapting to situations when necessary. And so, we need to pay attention to the leader's ability to be flexible from an internal standpoint, as well as looking at empowerment to be flexible from the organization standpoint as well.

Leadership Conformity
Conversely leadership conformity may have an influence on the infrastructure as well. And so, conformity in this situation does not need to be a negative item. It is not a total opposite of leadership. Flexibility. Rather leadership conformity looks at the level of risk and rewards that the leaders feel about a potential change idea and may look at the risk and rewards as being greater

in terms of change within existing ideas as compared to creation of new ideas. What this means is changes may occur within existing processes or changes might extend beyond existing processes to create new or novel methods incorporating these potential ideas.

EMPLOYEE INNOVATION – WHAT'S IN IT FOR ME?

We just addressed pieces of the Innostructure from the leadership's perspective. But one of the things that we as organizations fail to do is also look at the importance of innovation from the individual employee perspective. In other words, how do we help recognize employee innovation within the organization? How are employees awarded for their innovation? Conversely, how are they rewarded for their innovative ideas that may not come to fruition? These are things that need to be considered within the innostructure. The influence for this Innostructure needs to come from the organization within which will align with their core values and infused throughout. Three ways that the infrastructure can be strengthened from the individual's perspective is through the use of creative, educational and professional development opportunities for lifelong learning, from onboarding throughout the life of an employee, employee opportunity to be involved in leadership succession, as well as how folks are evaluated for innovation.

In summary, the first pillar of the GamiPHI Theory is the Play Potential. The three structures that need consideration from the perspective of the employee and the workplace are called infrastructure, equistructure, and innostructure. These considerations will lead to the employee's decision to engage in or disengage from the creative process in the organization. The next pillar that

Sandra D. Cleveland, Ph.D., RN

speaks to decision-making is identified as the Health Perception.

HEALTH PERCEPTIONS: THE STRUCTURAL ALIGNMENT DECISION

I'm a sports nut and have been an athlete (at least in my own mind) for most of my life. For a number of years, I have been working virtually (as many of us have experienced during the pandemic). As a result of working on a computer constantly, I have carried stress throughout my shoulders and back. When any of these issues cause me to struggle with tasks I normally do in my daily life, I seek out relief and see my chiropractor. Once I've arrived for my appointment, the chiropractor completes the necessary manipulations on the musculoskeletal system to put it back in alignment. As you're probably familiar, chiropractic adjustments help realign the bones and joints to relieve pain and increase the body's range of motion. But the appointment goes beyond that. They make the focus on the holistic aspects of health – so your chiropractor may recommend such things as nutritional or exercise advice to encourage a more health-conscious lifestyle.

Think about this in the context of establishing a healthy, creative work environment. When talking about structural alignment, there are a few things that individuals need to consider. As will be noted in the GamiPHI Theory explanation, the employee will have her/his perception of the three structures (infrastructure, equistructure, and innostructure). Additionally, the health and wellness of the employee needs to be considered.

EMBRACING PLAYER HEALTH AND WELLNESS

Before decision making can take place in the Health Perception pillar, employees need to consider their own health and wellness status as well as the three structures. Well-being is a more complex term that has been exposed to debates and criticisms. As a result of this, it would be hard to define what a doctoral student's well-being is in graduate school. Rather than focus on the definition, it seems better to center on what best describes a doctoral student's well-being. A vivid illustration would be Galvin and Todres' take on wellness in their conceptual framework consisting of "the Dwelling-mobility lattice" (Galvin & Todres, 2011). Here, they both state that well-being—independent of health and illness—can be experienced spatially, temporally, interpersonally, bodily, in mood and terms of the experience of personal identity. They believe that well-being is more complicated than health and is not restricted to any setting or role, e.g., workplace well-being or the role of being a student. Their definition focuses on the essence of well-being (Galvin & Todres, 2011; Todres & Galvin, 2010). Therefore, the best way to describe a person's well-being would be "the individual's experience of his or her health."

Well-being is a multifaceted phenomenon that has been studied in several different disciplines and thus has been defined in many different ways. However, it is common to use health as a starting point to understand wellness. The World Health Organization included well-being in its definition of health by declaring that "Health is a state of complete physical, mental and social well-being and not merely the absence of disease or infirmity" (WHO, 1948, p. 100).

The common theme of wellness is what builds the link between wellness and self-care. What are the themes? Proper diet, exercise, and stress-reduction techniques. The hallmark of a viable organization is the provision of comprehensive care at the workplace. Employees are taught to care for others (i.e., their customers); it is ingrained in their job description and purpose. However, comprehensive care centered on self is less prevalent for employees. Even with the short-term stress reduction programs and techniques that are reported in research, there are limited professional development opportunities that have been described to focus on self-care. No wonder employees often express reluctance to take the time required to care for themselves or find self-care activities that match their interests and that are easily assimilated into their lives.

The twist in this is that self-care reflects in the positive energy and vitality that can be brought to the workplace. And so, the lack of self-care cuts short the professional growth of employees and the sustenance to continue to care for others. One of the reasons why there is a lot of emphasis laid on employees caring for themselves as they care for others is because it addresses the reciprocal relationship between professional and personal growth. The quality of care provided for us affects your personal growth, and in turn, affects the quality you are trained to bring to the workplace. The quality of care each person brings to the workplace affects their professional growth. It complements the work of others too.

STRUCTURAL ALIGNMENT DECISION-MAKING

Once the perceived structures from the individual employee and organization are obtained, the person who is using this information, coupled with their health state, determines the level of alignment. In other words, we need to identify if there is structural alignment between the individual's perceived understanding of the differences in the three structures versus the organization statement on what their structure entails. The individual will gather the information of the three pillars (perceived infrastructure, perceived equistructure, and perceived innostructure) from both the individual and the organization standpoints.

Let's talk about the potential decisions the employee can make based on her take on the three structural pillars. If the employee believes that the three perceived individual structures and the three perceived organizational structures are intact, they will move forward to the next pillar (Innovation Potential) and start work through the 5-Is of the creativity cycle. The employees who fall in this category are your "go-getters" – i.e., they are the folks who are in the top 10-20% of the organization and are typically very engaged.

Action: Here's a caveat to pay attention to for this group of individuals. If there is no continual opportunity for personal and organizational growth, they may tend to feel ignored. A saying that this group of folks might use is "competence kills" …in other words, these may be the individuals that the organization consistently calls upon to get involved in different projects. Although these individuals may have intrinsic reasons for wanting to be involved, strategize how you might help recognize and reward creative contributions that align with the trajectory the employee wants to take. Make a conscious effort to periodically check on their take of the perceived individual and perceived organizational structures and their health and wellness when getting involved in different projects. Just because an employee perceived the structures were intact based on a previous project, the projected needs might change given the new project and context of the current workplace environment. Just because they perceived they were healthy and well during a previous project does not mean that they might feel stressed and early signs of burnout now. DO NOT IGNORE THEM. Once the techniques and communications are in place, monitor the employee for their perception of healthy structural alignment.

If the employee does not believe that the three perceived individual structures and the three perceived organizational structures are intact, they will stagnate and not move forward to the Innovation Potential pillar and work through the creativity cycle. The individual will have chosen to disengage from the organization figuratively – these are the individuals who are employed only for the paycheck and not moving forward with personal or organizational outcomes. The other option the individual might choose is to disengage from the organization in a more permanent fashion (i.e., attrition from the organization). This group of employees typically make up 10-20% of the organizational employees.

Action: This is where the bold arrows will come on The GamiPHI Theory – and where the strategies of CHROs, CLOs, and V.P. of Talent might move to a two-tier level of gamification and play direction. The bottom tier that the employee must work towards is meeting the role outcomes within a designated time frame. This will mean speaking to where the employee currently is – wanting to keep the job. Reiteration of the baseline knowledge and skills for the role might need to be readdressed. If the employee is unsuccessful in this quest, then the process of job separation must occur.

If the employee does start meeting organizational outcomes as outlined in the contract for the designated time frame, it's the time to move from the immediate to future contributions for themselves and the organization. The second tier then can move

114

forward from the survival tier to the thrive tier – that is, helping the employee start identifying personal, professional, and organizational goals to work towards in the next quarter, half year, and year. Strategically infused gamification and play methods can be used to move them beyond "here for the paycheck" to "here to _____" (it's typically an action they want to achieve). The goal is then to help them find their creative selves within the context of the organizational outcomes. Once the techniques and communications are in place, monitor the employee for their perception of healthy structural alignment.

What happens if EITHER:

- The three structures of the perceived individual are considered intact while some of the perceived organizational structures are not considered intact

OR

- The three structures of the perceived organizational structure are considered intact while some of the perceived individual structures are not considered intact?

OR

- The three structures of the perceived individual and organizational are considered intact while employee health and wellness is not considered intact?

Remember when it was mentioned that upwards of 85% of employees report being disengaged or highly disengaged, leaving 10-20% who are very engaged with and another 10-20% who are totally disengaged from the organization. Note that the large majority of your employees fall for this category. They are your steady workforce – they work hard to achieve personal, professional, and organizational goals. However, they may recognize (but not state) that there is an area from either the three perceived individual structures or their health and wellness state that impacts their willingness to fully embrace the creative cycle. They may be the folks who are increasingly taking breaks. They may express levels of feeling stuck, unchallenged, unmotivated, or unappreciated or they may not express it at all.

Action: The first thing that is important to recognize is their willingness to move creatively…but there is a disconnect between their personal "why" and the organization goals. Communication is the KEY to getting to the bottom of the employee's concerns. But recognize that communication without relationship building will probably be perceived by the employee as a cursory effort.

In nursing, we are often taught that the initial focus in an interaction with our patients should be active listening. This idea applies to any field. As a newer nurse, I tended to feel more comfortable with tending to the technical roles of the position such as monitoring the patient's heart, taking a patient's blood pressure, or educating a patient on their disease. What I did not do so well at that time was really hear what the patient was asking for without jumping in with an answer to what I perceived was their question. As a result, the patient might shut down some and wait until someone else would listen to them and address their real concerns. As a more experienced practitioner I really learned to be present with my patients. This is what your employees are looking for as well.

Start work with the employee to see where the issues are from their perspective. Is the employee not feeling challenged? You might explore the infrastructure issue – an example of this is the job description. When a job description states something like "and other duties assigned,' help the employee see how they get opportunity for assigned (or volunteered) duties that challenge her. Is the employee willing to even share their concerns? If not, you might explore her perception of organizational equistructure as the individual might not feel safe sharing the concerns without overt or covert retribution. As you work to find the issues, you can incorporate gamification and play for a number of purposes – as a way to open the communication pathway as a learning and development tool as a way to build reward into the activities. Once the techniques and communications are in place, monitor the employee for their perception of healthy structural alignment. Each employee will make a decision on their willingness to create within the organization based on perceived structural alignment and health. If the employee notes ill health or misalignment, you need to take measures to move him back towards structural alignment and subsequent engagement. Once the decision is made to engage creatively, the employee will move forward to Innovation Potential, the last pillar of the GamiPHI Theory.

The GamiPHI "Theory" Overview

Before I describe the GamiPHI Theory, please understand that the term theory here is not used in the scientific meaning of the word. Theory is typically defined in Merriam-Webster as "scientifically acceptable general principle or body of principles offered to explain phenomena." Rather, I speak to this in reference to a group of underlying principles towards a plausible composition of creativity. Some of the terms shared in the previous chapters are incorporated in the theory. Before jumping into The GamiPHI Theory, I want to briefly speak on the foundational concept of creativity.

What is Creativity?
Creativity is an intrinsic concept that nearly everyone finds hard to define. We can relate with creative people and the results of their creativity: Steve Jobs, the creator of Apple, Bill Gates, the creator of Microsoft, Frida Kahlo, a famous painter, and Thomas

Edison, the inventor of the light bulb. However, coming up with a definition that captures the concept entirely is difficult. I love the definitions shared by Ava Duvernay and Albert Einstein:

"Creativity is an energy. It's a precious energy, and it's something to be protected. A lot of people take for granted that they're a creative person, but I know from experience, feeling it within myself, it is a magic; it is an energy, and it can't be taken for granted."

~ *Ava Duvernay*

"Creativity is Intelligence Having Fun."

~ *Albert Einstein*

Don't you just love these definitions? They both speak volumes to me. Creativity is something we need to nurture in our businesses. Two assumptions that I made when writing it was that both organizations and individuals want to be creative. I want to briefly define organizational creativity and individual creativity, as you are going to be nurturing both:

Organizational creativity is defined as the making of a prized, useful new product, service, idea, or process by a group of individuals working together to achieve a common goal in a complex social system (Amabile, 1988). Organizational creativity is only valuable if implemented and adapted into the culture, ethics, values, structure, and processes of the organization.

We can define *individual creativity* as the use of a person's mind to generate something unique and original that is useful for people beyond the originator of the ideas (Amabile & Khaire, 2008). Every individual has the potential for creative abilities in the form of expertise (i.e., the knowledge an individual possesses that can be applied to his or her work in order to improve output), creative thinking (i.e., the capacity to judiciously garner the existing ideas and put them together in new combinations), and motivations (i.e., the need and passion for an individual to be creative).

The GamiPHI Theory aims to explain the factors underlying a healthy, creative organizational culture. It seeks to identify how an employee's perception of the organizational culture and practices impact their willingness to engage creatively. It's important to understand how the employee thinks their own perception of the work environment aligns with the organizational view. Alignment allows focus on employee and organization interaction during the creative process. The model emphasizes the roles that both the employee and the organization actively play for a creative environment and the opportunities to infuse gamification and play strategies that support a creative organizational culture towards innovation.

The GamiPHI theory is derived from a number of theories. One of the theories is Pender's Health Promotion Model. The basis for Pender's model is looking at how behavior is influenced by different factors. That is something that's going to contribute to the GamiPHI theory, because there is a health component that we need to pay attention to that we may not consistently address from an organizational perspective. The other theory that the GamiPHI theory is partially derived from is called the Organizational Culture Framework. This framework incorporates the concept of alignment. Note that the concepts of healthy culture incorporate gaming for purpose and play. Therefore, the gamification theory and the play theory are included as well.

What Does the GamiPHI Theory Mean for Organizations?

Understand that your employees are creating their perception of you and your business based on the components discussed in the GamiPHI theory. Your employees are constantly gauging the different types of structures that you have established in your business based on processes, based on treatment of individuals and teams, and based on the ability to *meaningfully contribute* to self and your business. They will use this check and balance system to determine if the business has a healthy, structural alignment. If they perceive that your business is healthy and in alignment, they are more likely to contribute. If they believe that your business is currently not healthy, they may be willing to identify opportunities to change themselves or submit ideas to the organization on ways that structural alignment can be achieved. As a result of structural alignment, your employee is likely to use their creativity.

INTRODUCING THE GAMIPHI THEORY

The following image is a schematic representation of the GamiPHI Theory. In this section, I'm going to discuss the GamiPHI Theory Overview. In subsequent sections, I'll expand on the pillars introduced and how they interact.

The GamiPHI Theory contains three major components (pillars) to the model.

- The first pillar is the Play Potential.
- The second pillar is Health Perception, and
- The third component is the Innovation Potential.

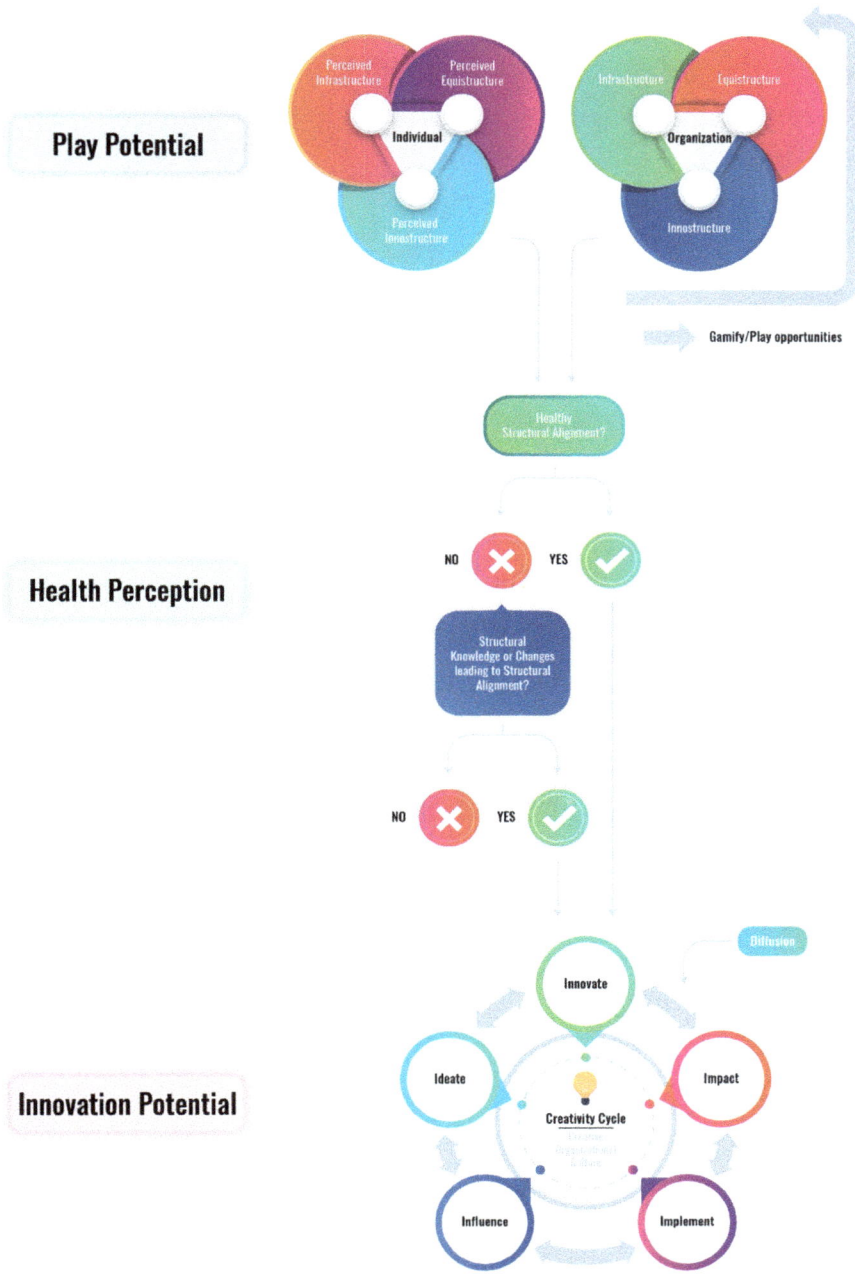

Figure 1. The GamiPHI Theory

Sandra D. Cleveland, Ph.D., RN

When discussing the GamiPHI theory, the big thing that is going to differentiate this theory from the previously discussed theories is the incorporation of play and gamification. Play, health, and innovation (the "P," "H," and "I") are where the PHI in the term GamiPHI is incorporated.

Pillar One: Play Potential
In the first pillar, (play potential), there are basically two perspectives that we need to pay attention to: the individual and the organization perspectives. When we were talking about play potential, I equate this to the understanding of what is involved with the playground such as what is involved with the rules (written and unwritten) and the culture of the playground. It's important to note both the individual (i.e., the players) and the organization perspective (i.e., playground keeper and monitors). Within the Play Potential Component, there are three similar *structures* from the individual and the organization's perspective. The different structure types are 'Infrastructure,' and I have coined 'Equistructure,' and 'Innostructure' (see Figure 2).

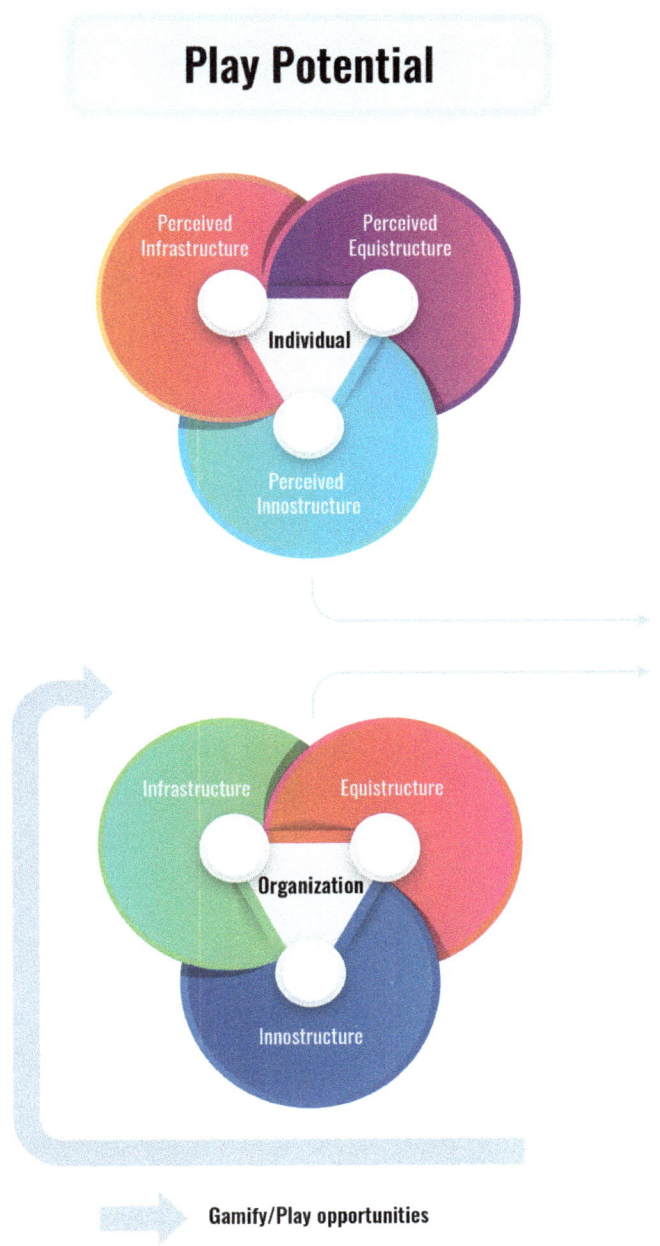

Figure 2. The Play Potential Pillar of The GamiPHI Theory

Sandra D. Cleveland, Ph.D., RN

Infrastructure, the first component, is defined by Merriam-Webster as "the resources (such as personnel, buildings, or equipment) required for an activity." It consists of human, technology, structural, communication, and other resources that help or hinder the functioning of the organization. Infrastructure is going to consist of items that are process-related -- what resources are available from the organization's perspective. Four items that will be described as the organizational culture, leveraging process and system processes, and risks and rewards.

The second component is *Equistructure*. Equistructure, loosely put, is the diversity, equity, and inclusion factor that organizations may or may not acknowledge at this point in time but understand the necessity of it. This addresses a portion of the perception of creative opportunity by each individual in the organization. Concepts of Social Determinants of (Organizational) Health, empowerment and psychological safety to support the equistructure pillar are included.

The final component in the Play Potential pillar Is *Innostructure*. This component speaks to the process used to move creatively towards innovation. Although many organizations strive to be innovative, innovation is not always attained. In the GamiPHI Theory, I contend that creativity is a perquisite to innovation and needs to be honed. This may be contributed to other factors hindering the occurrence of it. The organizational leaders affect the 5-I process (which will be touched on soon) – as a result, leadership involvement, leadership flexibility, and leadership conformity are tackled. Finally, the importance of infusing innovative practice and rewarding employee innovation is noted.

When discussing the infrastructure, equistructure, and innostructure, the focus is not only from the organization's perspective, but the perception of each employee within the organization as well. Organizations and their employees perceive the three structural components as it relates their creativity potential within that environment. The word perceived is noted for both sides. Even though the organization, for instance, may state that they have available resources, the individual may perceive that particular resource is unavailable to them based on their position or whatever factors (or vice versa). It's important to note both the individual and organization standpoints in terms of the play's potential, both of those come into play to the next stage, which is the health perception.

Pillar Two: Health Perception
Health is a big component that needs attention in our businesses. *The health and wellness of an organization is just as important as the health and wellness of the individuals who are within this organization.* In the GamiPHI Theory, once the perceived structures from the individual employee and organization are obtained, the person who is using this information to determine the level of alignment. In other words, we need to identify if there is structural alignment between the individual's perceived understanding of the differences in the three structures versus what the organization states on what their structure entails. The second pillar of the GamiPHI Theory is Health Perception and is represented in Figure 3.

Health Perception

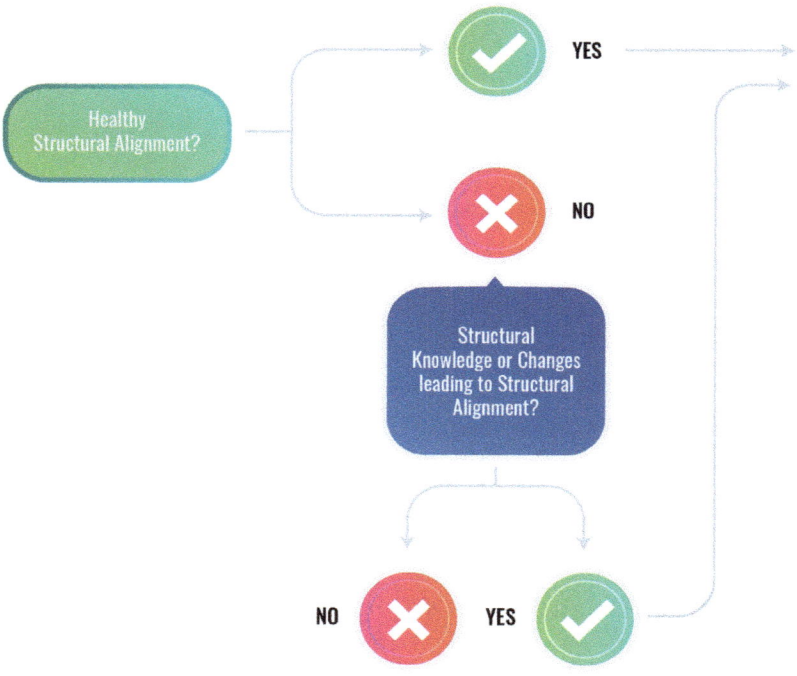

Figure 3. The Health Perception Pillar of The GamiPHI Theory

If there is healthy, structural alignment, you will see that it goes across into the Innovation Potential pillar...this is good because it means your employee is willing to share her/his gifts of creativity with you. If your employee perceives a misalignment between his/her vs. the organization's understanding of an issue, the employee may choose to temporarily disengage. You, as the business owner, need to identify if there is some structural knowledge or changes from either the organization or individual that need to take place.

Our goal here is to re-engage the person – so a feedback loop is brought back to the Play Potential to make adjustments to the structures. For instance, your employee may need to learn more about your employee benefits because they did not realize that it was already available to them and needed some knowledge related to that. Or maybe from the organization standpoint (that's you) you might perceive your current equistructure offerings as fair and equitable— but what they're delivering may not align with the employee experience, resulting in a change of policy or practice. Please listen when your employees are sharing their concerns with you! They are still at the stage where they are willing to remain engaged with you and the business. If your organization is considered to have a healthy, structural alignment, gamification can be used proactively to continue building on what has been working for you. If your organization is perceived as having some fissures in the alignment, there are opportunities to rebuild using gamification strategies.

Note: if a person stays stuck in the feedback loop, they may then choose (or the organization may identify) their lack of fit and move from disengagement to attrition. But if your employee perceives that structural alignment is intact, then we move forward to the third pillar called Innovation Potential.

Pillar Three: Innovation Potential

This pillar in the GamiPHI Theory moves the person forward from the willingness and perceived ability to be creative to a process of being creative independently and collaboratively. The five parts of the process are deemed the "5-I" creativity cycle: ideate, influence, implement, impact, and innovate. They take it through those cycles, and repeatedly take it through those cycles. It is not always linear movement; it can go back and forth based on some of the feedback they get (note Figure 4).

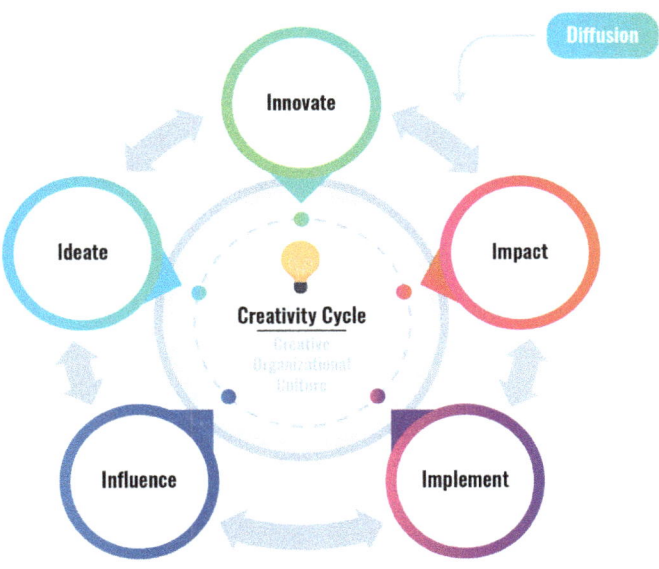

Figure 4. The Innovation Potential Pillar of The GamiPHI Theory

Ideate is the first stage of the creativity cycle. It is basically coming up with creative ideas. The person (or group) then needs to work through the organization, i.e., the influence. The influence stage is where stakeholder input and involvement are taken into consideration. The creative person needs to identify what influence they have within the organization and or the connecting bodies that they need to get aligned with for their creative ideas to move forward into action. Once they have influence needed, they then can work towards an implementation plan. Impact is the next stage. The focus here is identifying the formal evaluation pieces for the creative idea that has been put into place.

Typically, those are the four stages of the creativity cycle that most people will go through. It does not matter what level of employee is going through this process. because they may go through this creativity cycle based on an idea related to the floor. It may be an idea related to the department. It may be an idea related to the organization, but one of the key things that will take it from being a creative concept and moving it over into innovation is the concept of diffusion.

Diffusion will make the difference between a person moving through the first four stages of the creativity cycle versus through all five stages. Ladies - think about the opportunities you might have to diffuse ideas through your small business. For instance, can we try an idea in one department, refine it and attempt the revised idea not only in that department but others as well? Let's use a hospital setting as an example here when talking about diffusion. Questions we might ask to determine if innovation is occurring:

- Can we move the idea from the unit level to the department level?
- Does it diffuse through other hospitals?
- If it is a multi-system hospital, can we move it through other hospitals in the system?

Diffusion is the difference between moving ideas forward from creative ideas that impact the initially designed area to actual groundwork for innovation.

Conclusion:

This chapter on the GamiPHI Theory provides ways that you can identify the perceptions made by your employees and move proactively to address those concerns.

Here are some takeaways:

- We need to address the structures of infrastructure, equistructure (i.e. equity practices), and innostructure (i.e. innovation practices) built into our organizational culture.
- The way an organization makes an effort to play, stay healthy, and innovate are vital to both the employees and organization.
- Your employees may make a cognitive decision to mentally and/or physically disconnect from your business if they perceive misalignment between their views and your views.
- You can use gamification to address perceived misalignment or fissures in the structures.
- You and your team can identify organizational metrics speaking to the structures, play and health. This is important for buy-in of any gamified processes attempted in your business.

Do you see the possibilities to develop your gamified programs for the employees that can make you a thought-leader in the industry? The bottom line: there are a number of variables that we need to pay attention to, with one of the biggest variables being our employee's perception of the business.

Mastering the Metrics

For an organization to achieve success, it must first define what success is. Once the company outlines the business need that gamification can address, then the company can sufficiently outline its target outcomes and success metrics. The target business outcomes should be explicitly stated, achievable, realistic, and should be linked to success metrics.

Gamification comes in handy when trying to discover existing metrics in an organization. Since gamification is based on reward and progression, we can apply logical metrics to things that already existed.

"Business metrics: what you treasure, measure." This statement, paraphrased from a Margaret Heffeman saying, has a ring of truth to it. We need to understand that establishing your business metrics and assessing your business processes. Metrics and Key Performance Indicators (KPIs) are often used interchangeably. According to KPI.org, "[KPIs] provide a focus for strategic and

operational improvement, create an analytical basis for decision making and help focus attention on what matters most." Two important components of (KPIs) are *quantifiable measures* and *time*.

Input vs. Output KPIs

Simply put, input KPIs measure the behaviors that people are taking to meet the output KPIs, which measure results. But here's the thing we need to think about with this. If we do not identify metrics that mean something to the people whose behavior is being measured, the output KPIs either will not be achieved or, if achieved, will not be sustained.

It is important to actively involve your staff in creating the input KPIs. Equally important is creating and teaching employees about the vision for the organization and the output KPIs that will be used to measure the degree of shift created. Beware --crafting input KPIs from the top down will more likely lead to disengaged employees remembering input KPIs are based on behavior – if you want authentic behaviors developed, there has to be opportunity to self-define them. It is also important to note that the output KPIs tend to be lagging measures. They provide information on the efforts made after they have been made. It may take weeks or even months to receive and analyze the data. A potential advantage of using output data is the use of numerical values to measure progress. A potential disadvantage of using output data is that organizational responses tend to be reactive.

Input KPIs, on the other hand, can provide more immediate data to make necessary changes in the plan towards the ultimate goal. It can help provide some predictiveness to the results. Input KPIs might also incorporate more narrative data that supports or refutes the quantitative information, giving more perspective to the story that the data is telling.

Input KPIs can also be used to incentivize employee and leader behavior that is good. What do I mean by this? Let me share a quick example that Julie Zhou in an Adroll blog shared. In her example, she discussed a KPI towards Facebook's goal for every user to add "7 friends in 10 days." She further elaborates that it was a strong measure because it was easy to remember, could be quickly calculated, and encouraged those striving towards the goal to obtain "good" data- friends, instead of data that really would not mean anything "likes". A disadvantage is if the input KPI is not crafted correctly, teams may spend time trying to reach a goal that doesn't support the true goal. It's important that input KPIs are used in conjunction with output KPIs to provide a holistic picture.

But here's the issue. A lot of training and development efforts are directed towards meeting the *output KPIs*. What that means for your employees is that any effort that they put into place to contribute to the project is largely missed. If the team goal is not reached, employees have to wait for the data to be reported to get opportunities to ask questions and offer suggestions. That's why it's necessary to incorporate input KPIs from the employee perspective. Coaching opportunities for employees can be identified and implemented to address the input KPI and help ultimately meet the output KPI. Employees can then see more immediate feedback on their efforts and receive training and development opportunities directed towards the input KPIs. Your organization has big goals. Some of the goals tend to be defined more broadly such as "increase productivity". This is an example of an output KPI. However, the systems and people who are helping achieve the output KPIs need the knowledge and process to generate definitions using input KPIs. Play, health, and innovation (the three pillars of the GamiPHI Theory) can be infused as strategies for measuring both input and output KPIs. How does this look? The following briefly identifies ways to master the wellness, leadership, and innovation metrics. Why discuss these particular areas? Workplace wellness is receiving enhanced attention because many employees (approximately ¾ of individuals in various surveys) consider work-life balance a top priority. Innovation helps define your brand's worth and sustainability. Organizational leaders are tasked with moving forward these and other metrics effectively while satisfying customers and retaining happy and productive employees.

MASTERING THE LEADERSHIP METRIC

Many organizations are behind the 8-ball – being reactive vs proactive. According to the Business Insider, 83% of enterprises believe it's important to develop leaders at all levels in a company. However, that's not the case, especially for reactive organizations. Reactive organizations are shown to have:

- 38% of new leaders fail within the first 18 months (https://hbr.org/2018/02/1-in-5-highly-engaged-employees-is-at-risk-of-burnout)
- 69% of millennials believe there is a lack of leadership development in the workplace. As a result, companies continue to have workers churning. (https://bloomleaders.com/blog/2018/10/9/interesting-statistics-about-effective-leadership)
- It's costing you. The cost of attrition is large to replace these leaders. The Center for American Progress (CAP, 2012) conducted a study noting the cost of attrition was on average 213% of leader salaries. Organizations are having to replace leaders because managers may lack the necessary skills to handle certain situations such as crisis leadership.

The struggle is real for organizations to retain all types of workers. Managers with the best of intentions may not have the opportunity to hone soft skills such as emotional intelligence and crisis management. Wouldn't your organization love it if your organization could create proactive leaders? This is an opportunity to take the initiative and put a little play and gamification into the organization.

Identifying KPIs that speak to this issue are needed. If your leaders are struggling, they are either choosing to stay and tough it out but providing ineffective leadership or will choose to leave. By creating the output and input KPIs now, you are developing a plan that begins with the end in mind. Remember when I mentioned earlier those two components needed are time-situated and measurable? The KPIs identified as examples are briefly stated. For your KPIs, add those two components – this is the only way everyone will know if the goal has been met.

What *output* KPI(s) might be constructed from this example?
- Demonstrates leadership with clients
- A team 'health' KPI i.e., what is the pulse of the department?

What *input* KPIs might be constructed from this example?
- Achievement of 1 identified leadership goal

Please know that you can probably come up with many KPIs based on this scenario. However, it's not realistic to attempt to address all of them. You want to help leaders think about the results and influence they want to address and focus on KPIs that are reflective in measuring this. Now you have trained, competent leaders who are able to pivot and engage their employees.

MASTERING THE WELLNESS METRIC

Employee wellness is something that needs to be addressed in organizations. When it comes to keeping your employees well, many organizations are implementing wellness things so they can check the box – but often the proposed solution doesn't work. Studies have shown via Forbes.com (2021)…

- Presenteeism (poor productivity when physically at work due to wellness issues) can cost an organization 2-3 times the amount of a direct employee health issue.
- Successful wellness programs and healthcare costs can bring the average return on investment was 3.27
- Nearly 60% of leaders reported they feel used up at the end of the workday

What *output* KPI(s) might be constructed from this example?
- Employee engagement rate

What *input* KPI(s) might be constructed from this example?
- Are employees excited about the future for themselves and for the company?
- Satisfaction with any wellness programs in place

What is the return on investment? When you take wellness and add gamification as part of the strategy, it can then lead to low absenteeism, increased productivity, and the achievement of business and customer related metrics. Now you have well and healthy employees who are using their *whole* brain to contribute to the organization.

MASTERING THE INNOVATION METRIC

Are you an innovator? Where is your organization on thought leadership? Drop something in the chat that makes your organization stand out? Think about what the organization has done that's considered innovative or exciting. Although many organizations strive to be considered innovators or thought-leaders, the reality is that many organizations are behind the 8-ball – being reactive versus proactive. Proactive organizations are shown to:

- Subscribe to their thought leadership – your organization is the "go-to"
- People come to them for advice
- People come to their conferences for the new cutting-edge information in the industry
- 74% of buyers choose companies that first added value to their buying vision (SAVO, Techniques of Social Selling: Just Do It!, 2014)

I highly recommend reading *Case Study: Netflix shares "Netflix Culture: Freedom & Responsibility."* It's been read over three million times on Slideshare.

Wouldn't your organization love it if your organization could now cross over into thought leadership because you took the initiative to put a little play into the organization? Now you have employees and leaders who live the company's vision, considered innovators and industry leaders and are tapped for their insights, intelligence, and ideas -- they can be the best answer for your company's audiences. KPIs and metrics matter to different stakeholders throughout the organization. Make sure that metrics move beyond being project specific. Use the concepts in the

141

Sandra D. Cleveland, Ph.D., RN

GamiPHI Theory as areas to evaluate how a project impacts other departments and the organization as a whole. Please do not just collect the data and let it sit there. You and your project teams are identifying the IMPACT your proposed project has from the various stakeholder perspectives; ensure that data from the perspectives are being captured.

Cultivate Creativity
in the Organizational Playground

I have a confession to make. One of my newest all-time favorite movies is *Spiderman: Into the Spiderverse*. This newer entry into the Marvel movie franchise is based on a superhero story that many of us are familiar with. However, the absolute boldness in how the story was presented, and the twist of how the story's antagonist (Kingpin) collided alternate universes together. A Spider "man" from each of those universes came together – all with the exact same story line but of different races, genders, and even genres – but totally different individuals.

What was so utterly amazing about this film is that it offered the opportunity for almost every audience member to imagine themselves in the role of this awkward individual. The visuals for this movie were unlike anything this 20th century mom had witnessed before. I was chomping at the bit for the movie to come out after watching the previews for weeks and went to see it a couple of times. I was absolutely floored by the creative efforts, the storytelling, the EXPERIENCE. Think about all of the employees who helped to generate this movie, all of the hours it took to bring this idea together! The meetings to make sure the storyline, animation, voice characters all brought their best to the project. Think about how the human and non-human resources were used to bring about this piece. YOU are the connection to helping your employees understand the value of the organization, the value of who each employee is and what she/he brings to the proverbial table. You are the person who helps groups move towards the vision, even if they don't necessarily understand the full vision at the time. You are the person to help cultivate the ecosystem that is healthy, creative, progressive, data-driven, happy. In the Spiderman movies, Peter Parker (the alter ego of Spiderman) had an Uncle Ben who has the oft-quoted line I've used in previous chapters, "With Great Power Comes Great Responsibility". And it's true – you do have a lot on your plate. But one of the superpowers you have is the ability to provide the tools and resources to bring out the best in each of your employees. Which leads us to this portion of the book. Previously we focused on some of the foundational information needed to become a playful, creative organization. But here's the thing…

"Knowledge alone is not power – APPLIED knowledge is power."
~ Eric Thomas

We can talk about the knowledge all we want – this is a good step to establish the foundation of creativity that organizations strive to achieve in order to initially meet organizational goals and move towards innovation. However, it is necessary to take

ACTION…action to make the organizational playground, a healthy, inclusively safe, and play-worthy environment. Reading about the concepts is a good start – but the magic starts occurring when you start playing with the ideas. So, let's determine some ways you might move your organization members to engage and build their creative backbone using play and gamification by use of a case study. As you are aware, case studies allow us an initial way to apply the foundational terms and concepts learned to real-life situations. How do we translate the GamiPHI Theory into practice? *We need to make GamiPHI Theory based teaching, metrics, and incentives a core part of your healthy, creative organization.*

This involves a paradigm shift. It involves individuals at all levels of the organization to look beyond the immediate future and trends and define the shift and how play, health, and innovation is incorporated in the definition. And one of the definitions that an organization needs to process is their definition of SUCCESS in this new paradigm.

Review the following (imaginary) case study. Think about the case study from your current role. How might you introduce play or gamification strategies into the three pillars of the GamiPHI Theory? There will be some small examples shared throughout this section. Before you broach into this activity, know that the ideas I bring forth are not by any means "perfect" – and I'm totally fine with that. There is a lot of information in the case study that I may not have shared an example – but you can. Remember, part of the criteria for play is the ability to fail. Just because I suggest an idea and you try it; it does not guarantee success – at least if success is defined on getting it right the first time. Play is an opportunity to progress through the failures and try, try again.

"Play to progress, not to perfect." ~ Sandra Cleveland

Sandra D. Cleveland, Ph.D., RN

But this is the fun. This is where you experiment, think it through (but not too much), try, fail, and try again. Play and gamification is also social – so grab some others to float ideas. Figure out ways to help create a healthy creative organizational culture. Let's take a look at the case study.

CASE STUDY: PAY IT FORWARD – EXPANDING CORPORATE PROFESSIONAL DEVELOPMENT THROUGH SERVICE LEARNING

Introduction

Your corporation has been working in conjunction with Utopia University for two years. The corporation's role is to be a site where Utopia students can come and work in conjunction with your Community Partnership department to provide and connect with two local non-profits for service-learning projects. Utopia University has taken much pride in the service-learning projects completed by the junior and senior nursing students. It is becoming regionally known for the public service projects that are initiated by the students and sustained by the recipients of the students' efforts. As bell hooks states, *"What forms of passion might make us whole? To what passions may we surrender with the assurance that we will expand rather than diminish the promise of our lives?"* Students are increasingly able to connect the theory learned in the academic arena with the real-life practice they develop in the "field," and as a result, knowledge retention has increased and passion for public service is fueled.

What has been done in the past?

Historically, Utopia University representatives initiated the process of finding sites for student projects. On the other side, the

146

Community Partnership department would receive the requests and identify potential matches between a CP rep who acts as the mentor with the project site's representative. Some success has been shown with this method, but it was noted from all parties that the students might lose interest in continuing to make a difference in their local, national, or global community. While the Community Partnership department has noted these partnerships have brought forth some good projects, they have also noted that the program needs to be expanded and show evidence of effectiveness and sustainability.

This is where the Pay It Forward (PIF) project combined with the organizational philosophy that students can identify their own project, build, and complete a service-learning project that makes a significant change as identified by the non-profits and help the student and recipients continue to carry out the project.

These are the goals the collaborative is tasked with:

- Identify the strengths of the current PIF program
- Identify short, intermediate and long-term goals that will allow the Corporation and University to establish a sustainable evaluation strategy.
- To expose, teach, and get the "buy-in" of corporate administrators, team members, and faculty to service learning and the PIF program
- To refine the structure of the PIF program
- To develop a toolkit of evaluation instruments for the PIF program
- To develop training sessions about the chosen model and its applicability to the evaluation process.

147

Sandra D. Cleveland, Ph.D., RN

You are the chair for this collaborative project. You are given resources to expand your team so that there is a team lead for each of the goals. The end timeline for these tasks is nine months for the above goals – 3 months to roll out the revised PIF implementation.

PUTTING PLAY POTENTIAL INTO ACTION

Play Potential, the first pillar of the GamiPHI Theory, helps focus on the different structures that should be considered (and at times, acted on) to strengthen the likelihood that employees will choose to create in the organization. With this thought in your mind, let's look at how you (CHRO, CLO, V.P.) might take steps to strengthen the infrastructure, innostructure, or equistructure.

STRATEGY: DEFINE (OR REDEFINE) THE ORGANIZATIONAL PLAYERS FOCUS AND PURPOSE

In our case study, there are six goals identified for your joint project with Utopia University. Depending on your organization, you are in the position to either directly or indirectly assist with the organizing of the groups (I use mastermind groups here) and then assist them (if needed) to define the purpose of the group. Remember, you're not starting some sort of general support group that's applicable to all sorts of people. You're starting a group that will help a very specific type of process, issue, or product and focus on a specific mission.

First, start with the overall focus of your group. In other words, what is your group about?

- To refine the structure of the PIF program?
- Identify short, intermediate and long-term goals?
- Identify the strengths of the current PIF program?
- To develop a toolkit of evaluation instruments for the PIF program?

When choosing your focus, it is so important to find the right balance. If it's too broad, members may have wildly different goals. For example, if you create a mastermind around the topic of "fitness," some members may want to lose weight, others gain strength, and still others eat healthier. Let's use the first goal of refining the PIF program structure as an example. This particular goal is broad and would need objectives to assist with the identification of goals and how to measure success. On the other hand, if the topic is too narrow, it may be hard to generate enough conversation. For example, if you create a mastermind around the topic of "Using LinkedIn to Generate B2B Leads," there's only so much people can say. Try to find a topic that's broad enough to allow lots of discussion yet narrow enough so that people will be generally focused on the same thing.

Next, define the purpose of your mastermind group. Purpose can be broken down into:

- Mission. What are you trying to achieve as a group?
- Vision. What is the intended outcome of the group?
- Values. What actions and attitudes are valued within the group?

For example, let's say you created a mastermind group called "Growing the PIF Program through Online Marketing." The mission, vision, and values could look like:

- Mission: To help each other use online marketing tactics to grow our businesses
- Vision: That we would increase our sales, leads, customer retention, and other important metrics
- Values: Honesty, humility, a bias toward action, and a willingness to cooperate with others

By mapping these things out, you give your mastermind group helpful definitions. You clarify the objectives and spell out what sorts of things are expected from members. This, in turn, guides all the members in terms of what sorts of things are shared within the group, actions that should be taken, and more. Try to be as clear as possible when defining the focus and purpose of your mastermind group. The more clarity you have on these things, the easier it will be for you to manage the group. If you're not clear on your focus and purpose, it will be harder for you to determine which people to admit to the group, the sorts of things that should be shared, and the overall ground rules.

Example: "CREATE A TAT"
Let's say the group is focused on the vision statement to refine the PIF structure, but you want to move beyond sitting there and hashing out words as the sole activity. You could do an activity like "Create a Tat [tattoo]" that presents the vision in a visual format. This activity can be done in groups of 2 or 3. Emphasize that drawing skills are by no means required – stick figure drawings work just as well for this exercise. The individuals will then share among their group. The activity can then be repeated where a group tattoo is created. What you might find as a result of the activity is that the groups' key action verbs are discovered – and the values are infused in the explanation. Note that the groups formed should include representation from each organization (the

school, the non-profit, and your organization). Now that your team has an idea of the focus of the group, the actual KPIs need to be identified. Make sure that the KPIs are measurable and time oriented.

- What *output* KPI(s) might be constructed from this example?

- What *input* KPI(s) might be constructed from this example?

SUPPORT PLAYER SOFT-SKILL DEVELOPMENT

When I first started working as a hospital nurse, I felt comfortable in knowing how to deal with the technologies used to keep the patient's condition stable or help improve. Conversely, I also felt comfortable with the technologies if my patient's condition started to deteriorate. The IV pump – no problem. The electrocardiogram (EKG) that monitors the patient's heart – got it! My challenge was speaking to the patients and families. Even though it was touched upon in nursing school, communication with the families and fellow staff during the stressful incidents was a challenge for me. I often was initially perceived as rough around the edges. This also carried over into situations where I would perceive conflict. As I grew into my role as a staff nurse, I learned how to better listen more – and then respond to what was stated.

Sometimes employees may have an interest in being a part of a project but may worry about such things as having the ability to negotiate, connect with teammates, or share their critical thoughts. These are distinctly human capabilities that can be learned and applied while depending on little or no data to be performed: soft skills. Kenton (2021) defined soft skills as "character traits and interpersonal skills that characterize a person's relationships with other people. In the workplace, soft skills are considered to be a complement to hard skills, which refer to a person's knowledge and occupational skills."

Get to know some of the most valued soft skills currently in the job market:

- **Social Intelligence**: Ability to connect with others, to feel and stimulate reactions.
- **Cross-cultural Literacy**: Ability to operate in different cultural contexts and understand concepts in various disciplines.
- **Analytical Thinking**: Understanding data-based reasoning and knowledge of tools that aid in these analyses.
- **Critical Thinking**: Using logic and rationalization to identify strengths and weaknesses of alternative solutions, conclusions and approaches to problems.
- **Information Management**: Know how to discern and filter important information and understand how to maximize cognitive functions.
- **Emotional Intelligence**: Artificial intelligence still strays far from emotional management aspects. So, whoever has this ability to control complex situations will come out ahead.
- **Solver Mindset**: Ability to develop tasks and work processes for desired results.
- **Virtual Collaboration**: Ability to work productively and engage regardless of the platform.
- **Time Management**: Ability to self-manage and be productive in your activities.

- **Orientation to Serve**: Empathy and willingness to help others.
- **Negotiation**: Negotiation skills and reconciling differences are important for all professionals.

Example: Gamify soft skill acquisition

Let's say you're focused on the following goal from the case study: "Identify short, intermediate and long-term goals that will allow the Corporation and University to establish a sustainable evaluation strategy." Each employee involved in the team comes with a different skill sets. They may self-assess a need for increased efficiency in one of the soft skills that will allow them to be more effective in the development of the Corporation and University goals. Gamification could be used as a strategy.

Quick example? The power of text, time, and points achieved could be used here. The group leader can send out quick assessment questions to gauge the prerequisite soft skills of the group. Additionally, assessment questions directly relating to goal ideas could be posed. Points are assigned based on the quickest response (for instance, the first response back gains 5 points, the second response back gains 3 points, the third response receives 1 point). The assessment questions are sent at random times. Prizes can be given for the most points earned.

PLAY SMART: ESTABLISH YOUR PLAYGROUND RULES

Before you bring people into your mastermind group, determine some basic ground rules – i.e. (the playground rules). These rules clarify the basic structure and feel of the group. By establishing the ground rules first, you make expectations clear to potential participants. If people join your group without first knowing the expectations, they may either become unhappy or even back out later. Here are some ground rules to think about:

1. Meeting frequency. How often will the group meet? Which day of the week/month and at what time? What are the expectations in terms of attendance?
2. Meeting length. How long will each meeting be?
3. Meeting location. Where will each meeting be held? Will it be in a specific location or held online via video chat?
4. Preparation. Are members expected to prepare before each meeting? If so, what is involved and how long will it take?
5. Contribution. What things are members expected to contribute to each meeting?
6. New members. How are new members added? Who is responsible for approving new members?
7. Removing members. There may be rare occasions when it's necessary to remove a member from the group due to lack of commitment, breach of confidence, or other reasons. What process is there for removing a member from the group?
8. Size. How big will the group be allowed to get?

For example, Sara Christensen, Founder of Kickass Mastermind (considered one of the top mastermind groups in the U.S.), requires members of her mastermind group to sign an agreement with the following ground rules:

*   I will keep everything that is shared during the mastermind experience within the container of the mastermind unless I get express permission to share it outside of the group.

- I will give just as much or even more than I receive.
- I will receive with grace and without defensiveness.
- I understand this is not a group for self-promotion or pitching.

Be reasonable when you create these ground rules. Remember, employees have lives outside of the creative mastermind group. Be creative when creating the ground rules. Can this become an activity that incorporates play and gamification? Yes!

Example: Let's say you're focused on the following goal from the case study: "Identify short, intermediate and long-term goals that will allow the Corporation and University to establish a sustainable evaluation strategy." Gamification could be used in a couple of ways:

- To create the actual goals, participants can create a story and combine it with game elements, essentially creating their own "choose your own adventure" game.
- Level achievements in the game can correspond to the goals of the project.
- Taking this a step further, the employees can identify and create the actual badges that can be achieved.
- To assist with the sustainability of the project, add a badge towards "inspiring responsibility".

The goal for the group should help meet the project outcomes as well as personal/professional outcomes for group members. If you want people to join your group and benefit from it, it is important to have reasonable expectations. Once you've decided on the ground rules, put them into a simple document that can easily be shared with others. If necessary, you can always edit the rules in the future.

Sandra D. Cleveland, Ph.D., RN

PUTTING HEALTH PERCEPTION INTO ACTION

Health Perception, the second pillar in the GamiPHI Theory, focused on the decision-making process as impacted by employee's perception of the three structures vs the organization's perception. Additionally, the focus on employee health and wellness was a contributing factor that impacts whether or not a person is willing to move forward with the creative process for the organization. Let's review our case study. In the PIF Program, there are a number of companies who need to team up in the revision of the program (the University, the community partners [CPs], and your organization). When noting the infrastructure, innostructure, and equistructure concerns, note that all of the organizations need to be considered separately and collectively. For instance, if your organization and the University have a number of representatives at the meetings and the community partner can only provide one person, how will the group ensure the CPs are heard? This can be perceived as an infrastructure and / or equistructure issue, and ultimately impact the decision on how involved the CP might be during the process. If the CP feels unheard, it could impact their willingness to participate in future offerings of the PIF program – thereby ultimately impacting the University student experience.

Example: Foundation check
To assess if there are concerns in these areas (infrastructure, innostructure, equistructure, and health and wellness) build the proverbial building using labeled Jenga for each. Use a toy house to sit on top of the foundation (i.e., the Jenga logs). Every team member (and the team leader as well) will use a different color to label their 4 Jenga blocks, one for each term. When an employee has a concern in one of the areas, he will pull out the appropriate

brick and place it by the house. As you can envision, the more blocks pulled out, the more likely the foundation can crumble.

The goal: help resolve the issue. Is it training in a certain area that's needed? Create avenues for this to occur. Is the employee not feeling heard? Discuss ways that everyone has a voice. Conflict is inevitable as everyone has diverse opinions on the different parts or processes involved in the PIF Program or due to the different personalities around the table. When the issue is on the mend, replace the block back in the foundation. One instance of this – if the employee perceives their health and wellness is an issue, the workplace might need to remind the employee of available benefits or offer avenues to suggest new benefits. Some suggestions for wellness tools are listed below. NOTE: play and gamification are tools in your arsenal for engaging employees and cultivating creativity, but they are NOT the only tools. Some of the suggestions on the following list help display empathy for employee wellness, thereby creating a stronger relationship.

EMPLOYEE WELLNESS TOOLS

Regarding employee health and wellness, various devices are intended to improve your employee health and wellness. There is a wide scope of employee wellness instruments. Some of them are so basic – and generally modest – you may not consider them from the start, while others are completely digitized tech tools. Below, we'll take a gander at a couple of digital and non-digital models.

The Fruit Container
Presently, this regularly is one of those basic yet viable things that are not entirely obvious. The primary company I worked for used to have a fully natural product container remaining toward the

side of the two or three days per week. This is an exceptionally simple but not very expensive method of adding to your workforce's five per day! I generally was astonished to perceive the number of employees who got up one piece of organic product (frequently more) from that crate.

The Corporate Exercise Center Participation

Numerous organizations offer their employees an (impressive) markdown on an exercise center enrollment. While this may appear to be a smart thought – and don't misunderstand me – it's a positive development, but it doesn't work just as you'd anticipate that it should. In all actuality, it would appear it's normal for the most part those employees who go to the rec center effectively, paying little heed to the company markdown, that utilization the corporate enrollment. Another option, contingent upon your financial plan, could be an on-site practice office. Or on the other hand, if that is impossible, standing work areas, a ping pong table, and exercise balls.

Out of Office Time

A group trip can be an extraordinary lift for employee health and wellness. Once more, this doesn't need to be over the top expensive. Not exclusively are these off-site exercises a decent path for groups to become more acquainted with one another outside the work environment, they additionally are loads of fun! Consider laser-gaming, bowling, or trampoline bouncing, for instance.

Corporate Wellness Challenges

Onto a digital wellness device now. There are heaps of them, going from wearable technology and innovation to care applications and everything in the middle. The Outbreak is a simple illustration of how digital technology and innovation can make corporate wellness more fun. The game, created by A Step Ahead, is a group-based, six-week long advance and exercise challenge that gives employees the errand of making due in the cruel universe of a zombie episode. To endure, colleagues need to utilize true advances and active work. The advancement of the groups is followed, and groups are remunerated with rewards and additional focuses if they play well.

Regardless of whether you have a major or a little employee health and wellness spending plan available to you, there's consistently a decent digital arrangement out there for each organization.

Conclusion

The importance of proactive and periodic assessments cannot be emphasized enough. It can mean the difference between a team that gels and embraces the creativity of the individual and collaborative contributions. Or it can mean an employee choosing to disengage. Remember that in the GamiPHI Theory the bold arrows represent the opportunity to correct employee perception on structural or health concerns, which can then help the perception of structural alignment.

PUTTING INNOVATION POTENTIAL INTO ACTION

This is the second pillar in the GamiPHI Theory, and where the decision to become engaged and use their creativity for the common good of the project goals. Some employees may not believe they are creative and choose to stay on the sidelines for this reason. Or the employee does believe they are creative but are not challenged with using their creativity. The first strategy listed speaks to bringing out creativity in the individual employee. The next strategy speaks on forming creative mastermind groups to move projects forward. I also speak to creating the meeting background and tools to help move the groups creative endeavors.

STRATEGY: BRINGING OUT THE INDIVIDUAL PLAYERS

Tapping into Player Creativity ~ Do you love to be creative, but want to take your creativity to a whole new level? Do you feel overwhelmed by your work and find that your natural creative abilities and talents are untapped? If so, you need to learn how to tap into your creativity whenever you want or need to. *When you allow creative thinking to flow, you will find that you can enhance your natural abilities and accomplish more in less time.*

Creative Thinking Begets Creativity ~ Creativity allows you to become who you want to be. If you cannot release your creativity, you may feel your professional growth stunted, or you may not be able to think as clearly as you would like to. Many people don't realize the importance of creativity until they are taught to tap into it through creative thinking. Are you wondering how you can get started with creative thinking? You can begin with simple exercises like going through magazines and cutting out random images. You then can glue them all to a paper or a board without thinking about it – just let your creative juices flow! Finally, step back and see what your mind has created. You may be impressed and surprised with yourself. This surely will help you tap into your creative energy.

Listen to Something New ~ Another way to jump-start your creative thinking is by listening to music. Put on an album that you are unfamiliar with or borrow a friend's CD. *When you listen to something that you have never experienced before, you may find that you are changing your definitions of creativity and are lighting your creative fire at the same time.*

Get Creative by Getting Your Groove On ~ Dance! Creative thinking often starts with an active body. Put on a CD or go out to a jazz club. Try a dance class or enjoy the movement of your body in your own living room. Whatever it is, do something to get up and get going! You will be surprised at how creative you'll feel afterwards. You may feel inspired and ready to tackle new and exciting projects. Or perhaps you'll find that your workload isn't as daunting as it first appeared. After all, you'll be relaxing while having fun!

Write Your Heart Out ~ Another option is to set your timer for 15 minutes. From the minute you press start, you should write freely. Write whatever comes to mind without thinking about it or planning. Then step back and see the creativity that flowed from your mind to your hand, and then to your pen and onto the paper. Yet another awesome way to boost creative thinking is through affirmations. These positive statements can help you remember what it is to be creative and how wondrous it feels when creativity flows through you. You can create a list of affirmations for yourself such as, "I feel an intense flame of passion for things that interest me," that can help you tap into the creative person that you are, even as you deal with everyday stresses.

Conclusion

Organizations with a modern workplace culture understand that culture drives are not a one-time venture. Culture needs ongoing support. It is a liquid concept that is steadily changing, and continuously developing. Culture will only improve and stay relevant if those in charge pay careful attention to nurturing it. Organizations should routinely inquire as to whether the culture is effectively representing the values and objectives it intends. If it isn't, it needs to take action to get it back on track.

Organizations have an uphill battle to fight. The opposition for top ability is highly competitive, employees have high expectations for their managers, and innovation and quick advances in technology are changing how businesses function. The pace of progress is exceptional and unprecedented. When employees like and respect their workplace culture, their overall satisfaction increases exponentially. Giving your employees the ability to play, and offering them tools to find their authentic self, leads to increased employee satisfaction. If employees face a productivity-focused environment rather than a workplace that is supportive, they will find it difficult to be creative. Creativity is the key to the success of any business, whether it's developing exciting and innovative products and services or finding new ways to decrease costs. Creativity is vital. This cannot be emphasized enough.

Current employees are searching for reason, motivation, and connection in their professional lives. They want an advanced workplace culture that separates progressive models of power and advances straightforward leadership and group-based collaboration and connection. Organizations need to adjust, and they need to do it rabidly if they hope to survive. Where will you start?

Summary

We broached a conversation about the importance of organizational culture. The organization values should align with the social values and be infused throughout where it's transparent to employees in the organization and your customers. We touched on the ideas of creativity and engagement – what it is, what it means for employees and organizations, and strategies to encourage each. We spoke about the specific tools of play and gamification and the power of these tools to encourage employee engagement, help with productivity, and move creative projects forward.

We then moved on the discussion of the GamiPHI Theory, starting with a summary of the three pillars of the GamiPHI Theory – Play Potential, Health Perception, and Innovation Potential. Let's review:

Play Potential includes the infrastructure, equistructure, and innostructure, where the focus is not only from the organization's perspective, but the perception of each employee within the organization as well. Organizations and their employees perceive the three structural components as it relates to their creativity potential within that environment.

Health Perception is when the employee makes the decision to engage in a creative endeavor based on the perception of structural alignment of the 3 structures and perceived personal and organizational health and wellness. Finally, Innovation Potential is when the individual moves into the creativity cycle (the 5-Is). In this cycle, the individual/team moves through the process of ideation to impact. The creative product is considered innovation when it is diffused beyond the initially intended audience.

The culture of creativity begins with you and the leadership team. What you preach (and support with your practice, policies and procedures) all impact each employee as you all work to have a strong healthy creative environment. Each of you are part of the company's tapestry no matter what role you play.

BE THAT CREATIVE COMPANY

Please note that I did not really touch upon the companies who are known for the measures they put into place for a truly creative environment – but you know them and have heard of them before. We speak often of the Googles, the Apples, the Pixars of the world – and they readily deserve the praise heaped on them for being the creatives and innovators that they are. But let me share a last story on a company you may not have heard about – Kono Designs.

Kono Designs is housed in a nine-story office building based in Asia. They embrace architecture and environmental design – but they live it as well. Their website (http://konodesigns.com/635-2/) reiterates this idea. *When design unites the twin goals of improving life and business practice, it engenders beauty and crosses the boundaries of time to take on a life of its own.*

The environmental value is practiced not only for their customers, but for their employees as well. The building contains an urban farm inside the building, dedicating 20% of the building to green space. Employees are encouraged to maintain the crops – and they can do this during meetings! The food (over 200 types of plants according to Kono) is harvested, prepared, and served on-site for the employees, bringing new meaning to farm-to-table. I find this utterly fascinating. Don't you?

Here is my wish as you finish this book:

- BE the company that lives the values you promote.
- Be the company where employees absolutely love doing what they do.
- Be the company where embracing creativity brings about employees who are happy, healthy, and want to contribute to their own personal and professional growth as well as the company growth and bottom line.
- Be authentic and daring.
- Be phenomenal in the gifts you, each employee, and leader bring.

Now, go PLAY!

References

Organizational Culture: The Current State and Future Trends

Gray, P. (2013). *Free to learn: Why unleashing the instinct to play will make our children happier, more self-reliant, and better prepared for life.* New York: Basic Books.

Gray, P. (2012a). *Definition of play.* In Encyclopedia of play science. Retrieved March 19, 2022 from http://www.scholar pedia.org/article/Encyclopedia_of_Play_Science.

Gray, P. (2009). Play as a foundation for hunter-gatherer social existence. *American Journal of Play, 1,* 476-522.

Deterding, S., Khaled, R., Nacke, L., & Dixon, D. (2011). Gamification: Toward a Definition. Paper presented at the CHI 2011, Vancouver.

Katt, W.M. (2009). Facilitating Social Change Leadership Theory: 10 Recommendations toward Effective Leadership. Retrieved July 14, 2021 from https://journalofleadershiped.org/jole_articles/facilitative-social-change-leadership-theory-10-recommendations-toward-effective-leadership/

Sandra D. Cleveland, Ph.D., RN

World Economic Forum (Mar 2017). Technology and innovation for the future of production [white paper]. Retrieved on Jun 14, 2021 from http://www3.weforum.org/docs/WEF_White_Paper_Technology _Innovation_Future_of_Production_2017.pdf

Desilver, D. (2019, August 29). *10 facts about American workers.* Pew Research Center.

Lettink, A. (2019, Sept 17). No, millennials will not be 75% of the workforce in 2025 (or ever!) Retrieved on Jul 14, 2021 from https://www.linkedin.com/pulse/millennials-75-workforce-2025-ever-anita-lettink/

Harvard Business Review (2019). Crisis management: Signs your corporate culture is a liability. Retrieved on Jul 14, 2021 from https://hbr.org/2019/12/6-signs-your-corporate-culture-is-a-liability

Gallop (2021, Feb 26). U.S. Employee engagement rises after a wild 2020. Retrieved on May 12, 2021 https://www.gallup.com/workplace/330017/employee-engagement-rises-following-wild-2020.aspx#:~:text=through%20December%202020.-,After%20a%20rollercoaster%202020%2C%20U.S.%20employee%20engagement%20increased%20to%2039,while%2014%25%20are%20actively%20disengaged .

Society of Human Resource Management (SHRM.org). (May 11, 2022). Retrieved from https://www.shrm.org/hr-today/news/hr-news/pages/pandemic-missing-workers-ever-return-to-the-labor-force.aspx

BCBS (2019, April 24). The Health of Millennials. Retrieved on Jul 14, 2021 https://www.bcbs.com/the-health-of-america/reports/the-health-of-millennials

Kokemuller, N. (2021). How does HR add value to the organization? Retrieved on Jul 17, 2021 https://smallbusiness.chron.com/hr-add-value-organization-50980.html

Harvard Business Review. "A New Mandate for Human Resources." Accessed July 16, 2021.

The Cognizant Center (2020, Jun 25). An evolving profession: 21 New HR jobs to watch out for. Retrieved on Jul 17, 2021 from https://www.cognizant.com/perspectives/an-evolving-profession-21-new-hr-jobs-to-watch-for

Creativity

Amabile, T.M. & Khaire, (2008). Creativity and the role of the leader. In Harvard Business Review. Retrieved Jun 28, 2021 from https://hbr.org/2008/10/creativity-and-the-role-of-the-leader

Tang, M. & Gruszka, A. (2017). The 4P's Creativity Model and its application in different fields. In book: Handbook of the management of creativity and innovation: Theory and practice (pp.51-71).

Ideanote (2021). Individual creativity vs. organizational creativity [blog]. Retrieved on Jun 12, 2021 from https://ideanote.io/blog/individual-creativity-vs-organizational-creativity

Sandra D. Cleveland, Ph.D., RN

Amabile, T.M. (1988). A model of creativity and innovation in organizations. Research in Organizational Behavior, 10 (123-167). Retrieved on Jul 1, 2021 from http://web.mit.edu/curhan/www/docs/Articles/15341_Readings/ Group_Performance/Amabile_A_Model_of_CreativityOrg.Beh_ v10_pp123-167.pdf

Razumnikova, O.M. (2012) Divergent Thinking and Learning. In: Seel N.M. (eds) Encyclopedia of the Sciences of Learning. Springer, Boston, MA. https://doi.org/10.1007/978-1-4419-1428-6_580

Janis, I. L. (2007). Groupthink. In R. P. Vecchio, R. P. Vecchio (Eds.) , Leadership: Understanding the dynamics of power and influence in organizations (2nd ed.) (pp. 157-169). Notre Dame, IN US: University of Notre Dame Press.

Engagement

Gallop (2021, Feb 26). U.S. Employee engagement rises after a wild 2020. Retrieved on May 12, 2021 https://www.gallup.com/workplace/330017/employee-engagement-rises-following-wild-2020.aspx#:~:text=through%20December%202020.-,After%20a%20rollercoaster%202020%2C%20U.S.%20employee%20engagement%20increased%20to%2039,while%2014%25%20are%20actively%20disengaged .

Griep, R.H., Nobre, A.A., Alves, M.G.d.M. *et al.* Job strain and unhealthy lifestyle: results from the baseline cohort study, Brazilian Longitudinal Study of Adult Health (ELSA-Brasil). *BMC Public Health* 15, 309 (2015). https://doi.org/10.1186/s12889-015-1626-4

172

American Institute of Stress (2021). Workplace Stress. Retrieved on Jul 14, 2021 from https://www.stress.org/workplace-stress

McFeely, S. & Wigert, B. (2019). This fixable problem costs the US Businesses $1 Trillion. https://www.gallup.com/workplace/247391/fixable-problem-costs-businesses-trillion.aspx

Seppälä, E. & Cameron, K. (2015, Dec 1). Proof that positive work cultures are more productive. Retrieved on Jul 14, 2021 from https://hbr.org/2015/12/proof-that-positive-work-cultures-are-more-productive

Tools of Creativity and Engagement: Play and Gamification

Knowles, M. (1989) *The making of an adult educator: An autobiographical journey*(Ed.). San Francisco, CA: Jossey-Bass.

Merriam, S. B., Caffarella, R. S., & Baumgartner, L.M. (2007) Learning in adulthood a comprehensive guide. San Francisco, Ca: John Wiley & Sons.

Bureau of Labor Statistics (2017). Time use of millennials and nonmillennials. Retrieved on Jul 1, 2021. https://www.bls.gov/opub/mlr/2019/article/time-use-of-millennials-and-nonmillennials.htm

Petelczyc, C.A., Capezio, A., Wang, L., Restubog, S.L.D., & Aquino, K., (2017). Play at work: An integrative review and agenda for future research. *Journal of Management*. doi:10.1177/0149206317731519.

Sandra D. Cleveland, Ph.D., RN

Pelling, Nick. "The (Short) Prehistory of 'Gamification'..." Funding Startups (& Other Impossibilities), 6 Jan. 2012, nanodome.wordpress.com/2011/08/09/the-short-prehistory-ofgamification/

Katambur, D. (2018, January 8). *Why Gamification Works for Online Healthcare Training*. Rapid eLearning Blogs – CommLab India. https://blog.commlabindia.com/elearning-design/why-gamification-for-online-healthcare-training.

The GamiPHI Theory™

https://www.merriam-webster.com/dictionary/theory

https://www.merriam-webster.com/dictionary/infrastructure

Fortune.com (2021). Fortune 100 Best Companies to Work For® 2020. Retrieved on Jul 15, 2021 from https://www.greatplacetowork.com/best-workplaces/100-best/2020

U.S. Dept of Health and Human Services (2021). Healthy People: Objectives and data – social determinants of health. Retrieved on Apr 2, 2021 from https://health.gov/healthypeople/objectives-and-data/social-determinants-health

Edmondson, A. (1999). Psychological safety and learning behavior in work teams. *Administrative Science Quarterly, 44*(2), 350–383. https://doi.org/10.2307/2666999

Grant, A. (2014). Give and take: Why helping others drives our success. Penguin Random House, New York.

Clark, T. (2020). The 4 Stages of Psychological Safety: Defining the Path to Inclusion and Innovation. Berrett-Koehler Publishers. Oakland, CA.

Sinek, S. (2014). Leaders eat last. Penguin Random House, New York.

Rogers, E. M. (1995). Diffusion of Innovations (4th ed.). New York: The Free Press.

Rogers, E. M. (2003). Diffusion of Innovations (5th ed.). New York: The Free Press

Mastering the Metrics

Business Insider. (2018). U.S. workers suffer burnout when colleagues on vacation. Retrieved from https://www.businessinsider.com/us-workers-suffer-burnout-when-colleagues-on-vacation-2019-7?IR=T).

Center for American Progress (2020). The cost of turnover. Retrieved from https://www.americanprogress.org/wp-content/uploads/2012/11/CostofTurnover.pdf

Forbes.com (2021). Retrieved from (https://www.forbes.com/sites/edwardsegal/2021/02/17/leaders-and-employees-are-burning-out-at-record-rates-new-survey/?sh=7bf2d76e6499)

Sandra D. Cleveland, Ph.D., RN

Cultivating Creativity in the Organization

Kenton, W. (2021, Feb 25). What are soft skills? Retrieved on 7/20/21 from https://www.investopedia.com/terms/s/soft-skills.asp

Andrews, K. (2013, Sept 12). Pasona Urban Farm by Kono Designs https://www.dezeen.com/2013/09/12/pasona-urban-farm-by-kono-designs/

Rensselaer Polytechnic Institute. (2021, January 7). For the right employees, even standard information technology can spur creativity: New research examines the impact of IT on the front end of innovation. *ScienceDaily*. Retrieved July 20, 2021 from www.sciencedaily.com/releases/2021/01/210107125310.htm

www.ingramcontent.com/pod-product-compliance
Lightning Source LLC
Chambersburg PA
CBHW051521120626
46551CB00012B/1029